CHRIST
THE MEANING OF
HISTORY

CHRIST
THE MEANING OF
HISTORY

by

HENDRIKUS BERKHOF

translated by
Lambertus Buurman

BAKER BOOK HOUSE
Grand Rapids, Michigan

Translated from the Dutch, *Christus de zin der geschiedenis,*
4th ed., G. F. Callenbach N. V., Nijkerk, 1962.

Library of Congress Catalog Card
Number: 66-11503
ISBN: 0-8010-0762-3

PHOTOLITHOPRINTED BY CUSHING - MALLOY, INC.
ANN ARBOR, MICHIGAN, UNITED STATES OF AMERICA
1 9 7 9

If history has been fulfilled, but still continues, how and when will it end? And, since it must continue, what is its significance until it ends? There are beginnings of answers to those questions in the New Testament. Perhaps even the full answers are there and Christians are too slow in discerning them.

John Marsh, *The Fulness of Time*,
London, 1952, pp. 121f.

CONTENTS

PREFACE TO THE ENGLISH EDITION

THIS BOOK was published in the Netherlands, in the Dutch language, in 1958. It went through four reprints. Some substantial changes were made for the third edition (1959) but the fourth was just a photomechanical reproduction. Thus seven years have passed since the last revision, years in which much important literature on the relation of Christ and history has been published, though there has not appeared, so far as I know, another book with the same scope and covering the same field. These two facts do not exclude one another, because the theological climate of these years was unfavourable to endeavours like mine: in this period the convictions underlying the central New Testament chapters of this book have been under heavy attack from the school of Rudolf Bultmann.

Were I to have to write my book now, the approach would be rather different. However, it is impossible for an author, at any rate for the author of this book, to rewrite his book after seven years without losing in freshness and substance while gaining in theological exactness and timeliness. So I decided to leave it as it was, with some slight necessary amendments, but to add a short Epilogue for theologians, to inform them of my position on this battlefield. As a consequence of this I felt free to remove quite a number of footnotes which referred to older publications.

H. B.

FROM THE PREFACE TO
THE THIRD DUTCH EDITION

I MUST first give expression to my surprise and gratitude. This book has been received with a response far beyond my dreams. It has been read widely outside the circle of theologians. More than one reader assured me that the book had given him courage to live and labour on through the wilderness of secularism. A higher reward than this assurance is not possible for an author.

Perhaps the reactions of the theologians were most surprising to me. The book moves far away from the theological highways of our time, and I had counted on rough verdicts of rejection. So far this has not been the case. On the contrary, several theologians whose judgments I value highly expressed their appreciation either by letter or review.

All this proves not so much the quality of my book, as the questions that are alive in the Christian Church today. In reaction to the way in which the theology of the nineteenth century tied together Word and reality we have separated the two sharply. This may lead to losing the connection between them. The Word then becomes an abstraction and reality is secularized. Therein lies the fundamental problem of today's theology, and *the* problem for today's preaching. I attribute the response to my book to the fact that it tries to put in words the continuing mutual involvement of God's actions and words, and what we call our reality. If we truly wish to serve man with the *Tat-Wort* of Revelation, then precisely here, without drowning in the nineteenth-century questions, we theologians must lay aside our hydrophobia.

INTRODUCTION

When we can no longer find meaning in history it means that
we do not understand ourselves.

G. van der Leeuw, *De Zin der Geschiedenis*, Groningen, 1935, p. 5.

AGAIN AND again, more and more, we are assured that we
live in an apocalyptic era. The question is whether those
who say this know what they mean. If it is more than the
assertion that this era sets before us surprises and fears that
have never been seen before, then it must mean that we live
in an age that more than any previous one unveils (*apo-
calypsis* means 'uncovering'); a time in which the great
forces that move human history are unveiled from their
mystery; a time that sees to the end. In this assurance, then,
we are dealing with one of the many sighs, so freely sighed,
which prove how much our Western world still lives by its
Christian heritage, and how much we unconsciously orient
ourselves by it when we seek a way out of the events which
overwhelm us. Probably this last phrase is still much too
mild to express the real problem. Our generation is strangled
by fear: fear for man, for his future, and for the direction
in which we are driven against our will and desire. And out
of this comes a cry for illumination concerning the meaning
of the existence of mankind, and concerning the goal to
which we are directed. It is a cry for an answer to the old
question of the meaning of history.

The Church of Christ not only knows of such a cry, but
also knows of a divine answer. She must set herself alongside this world and must dare to point to the answer. The
question, however, is whether she is able to do this. She

certainly stands alongside the world, or even completely in it, for she also is strangled by fear. But she can only be of solid and real help when she is able to bring an answer out of her own and others' fear. This she can actually do because her book, the Bible, is full of light, precisely for these abysses of history. There the building materials are piled up high for what we may call a *theology of history*.

But for many centuries the Church and her theologians barely noticed these materials. A few words have been said about the so-called 'signs of the end' in a hidden passage in the dogmatics, somewhere near the end. Usually the passage has been very sombre and has dealt entirely, or almost entirely, with the increasing evil of man and the coming antichrist. A few observations in this passage used to point to the possibility that what had been said might touch upon the core of world history, including the history of the present. But the hiddenness of the passage, the brief treatment afforded, and the localizing of facts in an uncertain future, have resulted in a situation where these 'signs of the end' remained as lost stones in a dogmatic field, and the building materials needed for a theology of history were not gathered.

This does not, however, include all who call themselves Christian. Throughout church history the quest for a theology of history has been important to sects and sect-like movements. One finds here a clear and detailed answer that satisfied not only faith, but also curiosity and primitive intellectualism. This while the official church had no answer at all.

The relationship between the churches and the sects has for this reason also been fruitless. The sects have reacted against the cool attitude of the Church to the questions that touched on the future and history, and the churches have reacted against the fantasies and sometimes revolutionary outbursts that have been evidenced among the various sects. Every response has called for a new response, and the questions for a theology of history have been approached either not at all, or in a fantastic and dilettantish manner. There has seemed to be no third possibility. One could say that since there are only two alternatives it is best to choose the first. But no attention is as disastrous as a wrongly directed attention. Many Christians, who in spite of the riddles and sorrows of their personal lives do not lose the assurance of God's love and guidance for a moment, feel themselves as defenceless and helpless as lost children suffering from the absence of the Father, when they read the headlines in the newspapers. The twentieth-century Church of Christ is spiritually unable to stand against the rapid changes that take place around her because she has not learned to view history from the perspective of the reign of Christ. For that reason, she thinks of the events of her own time in entirely secular terms. She is overcome with fear in a worldly manner, and in a worldly manner she tries to free herself from fear. In this process God functions as no more than a beneficent stop-gap.

Fortunately there are signs of change. These are only small clouds, the size of a hand, but they are visible. The experience of the Second World War has helped push in this direction. The Reformed Synod's document, *Fundamenten en Perspectieven van Belijden* (Foundations and Perspectives of Faith), has gone beyond the confessions of the sixteenth century by including an article about history (art. 14). And the World Council of Churches had as its theme for the Evanston conference in 1954, 'Christ—the hope of the world'. The well-known report regarding this theme which was accepted by the assembly contains a paragraph entitled 'The Christian Hope and the Meaning of History'. These things are symptomatic and gladdening, even if the content itself is at this point not satisfactory, particularly in the case of the second document. But we have only just started. There will need to be much more thinking on this subject. Only then will our talk about Christ's reign in history slowly begin to have meaning because it will approach more nearly the fulness and certainty with which it is spoken of in the New Testament.

It is my desire and hope to help this process with this

book. I hope for no less and I expect no more, for it has been strongly impressed upon me that we have here an uncultivated theological field. This is, however, the legacy of history. Since dogmatics kept itself systematically removed from the problems presented by the apocalyptic books of the Bible, I was often forced to find my own way without the aid of this tradition. For this reason, among others, I remained as close as possible to biblical theology. This does not remove the fact that one cannot make pronouncements in this field if one is not also prepared to come close to a Christian philosophy of history. He who fears the latter cannot do justice to the biblical pronouncements. But for this same reason it has become a somewhat strange book in which exegesis, biblical theology, dogmatics, and philosophy change places, and at times even intertwine. For someone like myself, who is not a specialist in any of these fields, this has been a perilous undertaking. Fortunately some specialists have been willing to read a few of the chapters and point out some necessary corrections. To them I express my sincere gratitude.

Theology is a form of loving God with the mind. For that reason it is not a secret doctrine but a public matter. Thus I have considered it a pleasant, self-imposed task to write in such a way that non-theologians with a general intellectual orientation can read this book. I trust that many of them will wish to do so, for it is important that the matter discussed in this book start to come alive to the whole Church of Christ, as much-needed bread. It may be that even those who count themselves among the sects may wish to become acquainted with this book. They will find it inadequate, and will disagree with much of it, but perhaps they can appreciate it as a work by someone who has heeded their knock at the door of the Church. And there may be a slight possibility that it might lead them to ask where the reactive elements are in their own teaching. At any rate I trust that this book may be a small bridge across which Church and sects can find a way to a new dialogue.

I

ON THE MEANING OF EVENTS

The horizon of archetypes and repetition cannot be transcended
with impunity unless we accept a philosophy of freedom that does
not exclude God.
Mircea Eliade, *The Myth of the Eternal Return*, trans. W. R. Trask,
New York (Pantheon Books), 1954, p. 160.

WHOEVER WOULD discuss the meaning of history must
first set forth in clear language what he understands it to be.
History is the study of man's actions and decisions. It is the
terrain on which man's cultural mission is realized; along
with this it is also the terrain of his self-realization. What
we point out in these words may be said to be the meaning
of history. This, then, is what many understand by the
word 'meaning'. One can also think of this term in connection with the way in which the diversified events of mankind
stand in relation to God—how he holds these in his hands
and how he uses men and things. In this study we understand
the word 'meaning' in a third, more narrow sense which in
European culture is very common, but which presupposes
and goes beyond the other. We understand 'meaning' in the
sense of 'goal' and of the movement towards it.

Have human events throughout the centuries had a speci-
fied direction, or have they been in an up-and-down movement without coherence? Is there a thought behind events
in their succession? We Westerners happily use the idea that
history is like a stream moving toward a specific point. We
see it not as a sea without shore or form, but as dammed up,
streaming to a known or presumed goal. This realization
has largely determined our life, and by it Westerners have

17

become what they are in the midst of their fellowmen—active, *zielstrebig*, and idealistic. This book concerns itself with the faith in the meaning of history which, consciously or unconsciously, is the spawning ground of this attitude.

Emancipation from the Cycle

The concept of history as a stream is certainly not universal. We do not find it, for example, among primitive people, or in most of the ancient cultures. Man of those periods experienced human existence as a part of the events of nature embedded in the natural law of rising, shining, and setting. The wide difference between nature and history by which we live was not known, or at best unclear, to these people. Although we find feelings of longing for a lost state of happiness, and expectations that this paradise will one day return, we find that these have no influence on the experience of human events in the time between. These events take place in an eternal *cycle*, even as everything else in nature. In Hinduism things are different only in that human events, and events in general, do not receive a metaphysical meaning, except in the negative sense that it is *maya*—a *veil* over eternal, unchangeable Being. It is not surprising that what we call an elementary recognition of a 'sense of the past' is barely present in Eastern cultures.

This naturalistic experience of events, however, is not the last and only thing to be said about the ancient cultures. Jaspers introduced the term 'axial period' (*Achsenzeit*).[1] This is what he calls the last thousand years before Christ when almost simultaneously, but without connection, a new spirit arose in the leading cultural groups in China, India, Greece, Persia, and Israel. Then man no longer experienced himself as a function of the harmonious cycle of nature. He came to stand against nature; he emancipated himself; the critical sense awakened; 'being human' was discovered in its own individuality. During that period the foundations were laid for world history which began about AD 1500, according to Jaspers. With this concept Jaspers introduced a useful

18

idea. The question arises, however, whether, geographically and historically speaking, he considers these periods in too strict a sense (is it proper to exclude Egypt so rigorously?), and, on the other hand, whether he overstates the variations in origin of China, India, and Persia, as far as their historical significance is concerned. But it is certain that we do not see an emancipation from naturalism only in Greece and Israel, and it is good that Jaspers widens our vision at this point.

Such an emancipation from naturalism does not necessarily mean that history is now understood as a movement toward a goal, even though the reverse is true—the latter is impossible without a break with naturalism. In China and India it did not result in a new concept of history. Persia was a different story. Zarathustra, whose half-legendary figure is the middle point and symbol of the cultural break that took place in Iran, saw events as the scene of the struggle between light and darkness, good and evil; a struggle which continues through several eras and ends in the total victory of light; in that struggle man is called to choose the right side. Here we can speak of history in terms of our suggested definition. But I must not press this point too far. The documents of Zoroastrianism are dated from a much later period, and the original prophetic vision of Zarathustra was eventually overshadowed by the naturalistic idea of the cyclical course of history. At any rate, in Persia, it did not come to a new and culture-building experience of history.

Greece and History

Although naturalism remained as an undercurrent, in Greece the break with naturalism was much more radical. Nowhere else has the autonomy of man against his surroundings been experienced in this way. Here were uncovered treasures of 'being human' which to this day we have not ceased to admire. Among these treasures belongs what we call the 'sense of history': namely, the ordering of what has happened in the world, in the service of the determination of our place in the present. We may thank the Greeks for this sense of history. Herodotus, Thucydides, and Polybius brought this sense of the past to the attention of future generations and cultures. This is how we learned to see ourselves as coming up out of the coherence of actions and thoughts of the past, and as walking into the future.

Yet the Greeks, differing from Zarathustra, have little if any sense of history as events leading to a goal. Such a concept did not suit the Greek mind. The Greek seeks for the perfect, which to him means that which exists in itself— static harmony. Thus perfection and harmony cannot be found in changing events. The finite has as such no eternal meaning. At best one can say that the eternal is reflected in history, sometimes more, sometimes less, but always in a broken and distorted form. History itself is ignorant of what it reflects. It is capricious in its ups and downs, at bottom arbitrary, and, in the end, ruled by a dark Fate.

It is often said that the Greeks also thought of history as a cycle. In general this statement is not correct; but however history may have been seen, it had no meaning; for time in itself has no part in the eternal, and hence has no meaning. To the Greeks, the passing of time is primarily experienced in a negative and pessimistic way. Whoever says, 'Time', also says, 'Transitoriness'. This is sufficiently proven by literature, particularly the lyrics. Only one philosopher, Heraclitus, has made 'becoming' the starting point of his thinking. But he knows nothing of progress either; he in particular speaks about a cycle. To him history is a wedding of Up and Down, and despite all dynamics is, at bottom, a static unity of contradictions. And it must even be said of Greece's most copious and stimulating thinker, Plato, that he could see in history no more than imitation and remembrance of 'The Idea'. The Greek had no view toward the future; his interest in history was directed to the past. Although there may have been exceptions, especially in the creative fifth century, they remain exceptions. The determinism of the Stoic and later mystical philosophy are also a-historical.

On the Meaning of Events

More than any other people before them, the Greeks discovered in man a being that transcends the events of nature. With them, man creates for himself an ideal, timeless world. There is no room here for history. This world of ideas can reflect itself in history, but the latter does not stand above nature in principle.

Israel and History

We must thank not Greece, nor Persia, but Israel for our sense that history is goal-directed, and that as such it has meaning. In that same fruitful axial period (long before its beginning, according to Jaspers), there originated an entirely new type of historical realization—also different from the Greeks'—a realization that directed itself not only to the past, but also, guided by the past, to the future. The documents make plain the fact that this unique variation of origin with regard to naturalism stands in indissoluble connection with that distinct God who on behalf of his people intervened in the events, and in this way turned events into a guided history. At its beginning stands Abraham as an example and symbol, called from the astrological naturalism of Ur, and started on his way to Canaan. Only when he arrived there was he really on his way to a future that would involve all nations (Gen. 12.1-3).

> A voice broke through the silent circle
> Of the existence of which he was
> A part; he is straightway
> Shuffled into the long journey
> On which he henceforth shall go.[2]

God delivers his people from Egypt; he makes a covenant with them; he leads them through the wilderness to the promised land, and in that land he prepares them by guidance and grace for the important day when they will live entirely by his law, and when they will be a blessing to all nations.

In Israel, man is emancipated from nature by the Word

which asks for a definite answer, and then goes before man
through time, pointing the way. In this way history is freed
from nature much more radically than in Greece. There is no
cycle. Nor is there chance, or an inflexible fate. History is
the terrain of human freedom and responsibility because it
is primarily the terrain of God's calling and leading. Man
is delivered from nature because he is delivered by and for
God. Thus he is set upon the road toward the great object
—the Kingdom of God.

This idea becomes central in the New Testament. There
the cry sounds, 'The kingdom of God is at hand!' The
promise of that kingdom as the goal of history is now realized,
i.e. firmly established. This realization began with Jesus.
The end time has now arrived. His life and sacrificial death,
his words and miracles, all united in his resurrection and
glorification, rang in the last phase of history. The boundaries of Israel are now torn open, and the Gentiles take part
in the salvation of Abraham. History has now not only a goal
(the return of Christ), but also a centre (his first coming).
The believer looks forward and backward, and knows himself to be involved in the unrestrainable movement towards
the completion of God's Kingdom.

Some Christian Views of History

This unknown sense of history, originally present only in
a few small groups in the Roman Empire, has especially
since the fourth century influenced the classical culture, and
later to a larger degree the nascent spirit of the Germanic
peoples. Many views of history have grown out of this
realization. The first of importance was that of Eusebius of
Caesarea set forth in his *Historia Ecclesiastica*, during the
time of Constantine the Great. History before Christ was
preparation for his coming, while the glorious fruits of his
appearing have only now been revealed in the messianic
figure of Constantine; the time of salvation has now arrived
that was expected in the Old Testament, upon which will
follow later the actual kingdom.

But the great Christian philosopher of history was Augustine. His main work, *The City of God*, is to this day the classic Christian view of history. The Middle Ages, and the Reformers particularly, were led by it. Alaric's attack on Rome, in August 410, dealt the death-blow to the traditional, proud, Roman view of history that human events were dated from the establishment of the eternal Rome, *ab urbe condita*. Augustine, who wanted to prove to the embittered Romans that the end of their empire was not due to the revenge of the gods for the neglect of their cult by the Christians, but that it was to be blamed on their own heathen vices, did in fact much more (especially in the second part of his work, books 11 to 22). In place of their lost opinion of history he gave them a new one that would be proclaimed by the centuries. For Augustine the meaning of history is found in the struggle between the earthly and the eternal kingdoms. The worldly states, personifications of the earthly kingdom, will be destroyed in a vain cycle; the Kingdom of God will go through strife to meet her glory. The millennial kingdom was initiated by the coming of Christ; in this kingdom the Church reigns and exercises her right of binding and loosing.

Augustine's large work provided the framework in which the following 'Christian centuries' moved when thinking about history. Even the Reformation simply accepted it, and renewed it wherever humanism had moved it aside. The Reformers, however, were generally very careful in their expression of history from this perspective. They were discouraged by the way in which the Anabaptists interpreted history in connection with the Kingdom of God, and particularly by the Anabaptists' view of their role in the Kingdom of God, which they zealously tried to fulfil (Münster!). For that reason Calvin did not write a commentary on the Revelation of John. Luther expressed himself very critically in his introduction to Revelation in 1522. Yet he did not shrink back from a strong topical interpretation of Revelation in his new introduction of 1530. Although the Reformers were afraid of sectarian interpretations, they, like the Middle Ages, were convinced that history moves between the Fall and completion, that Christ is the centre of this, that we are involved in the struggle between him and evil, and that he will gain the victory in that struggle. This view of history has for centuries been typical for Europe; indeed, it made Europe, and gave seriousness and direction to the actions of Europeans.

Idealistic Views of History

But it has not remained this way. In the leading circles of Europe, entirely new philosophies of history have cropped up since the middle of the eighteenth century. A typical document representative of this is Lessing's essay, *Die Erziehung des Menschengeschlechts*, published posthumously in 1780. In this brief masterly essay, Lessing suggests that the history of man is a training period in the ways of God, in which revelation serves to reach a future phase more rapidly than is possible by reason alone. The development is from lower to higher; the higher the stage, the less Christian revelation in the traditional sense is necessary. The final goal is reached when man has become of age, and is led solely by his reason to do good for the simple purpose of doing good. Then the time of the 'eternal gospel' will have arrived.

This brief essay marks the transition to a different experience of history, among the intellectuals of Western Europe. The Christian view of history as a struggle between two kingdoms, followed by the victory of Christ, gives way to a view in which the struggle is replaced by *development*, and in which history is not moved by the contradictory forces of God and evil, but by the good forces God has placed within man. One may characterize these opinions, which were not without incidental predecessors in earlier centuries, as immanent, evolutionistic, and idealistic. Soon after Lessing, his point was discussed much more eloquently and with better arguments by Herder. Herder sees *humanity* as the final goal of God's dealing with mankind. The great philosophers of German idealism, especially Hegel, pursued this thought further. It is clear that we are dealing here with a concept that is opposed to the Christian concept of history. Yet, we must say, when we consider this movement from our distant vantage-point, and when we know by what opinion it was replaced, that, in its own secular way, it drew from the Christian witnesses. It considered history not as a cycle, semblance, or accident, not a process of nature, not mere events, but as (immanently) goal-directed, driven by a plan, moving to a future of bliss. Only in a Christian-oriented culture could this concept be possible.

Positivistic Views of History

Soon many totally different opinions of history began to interest the leading minds; opinions which we may characterize as deterministic, naturalistic, and positivistic. While idealistic systems were developed mainly in Germany, the naturalistic systems often came from France and England. In the leading European circles these concepts, after 1830, began more and more to overshadow the idealistic systems. The master of this tradition is Auguste Comte with his six-volume *Cours de Philosophie Positive* (1832ff.). He argues that man develops according to fixed, social laws which are the continuation of the biological laws of lower nature. In this development the intellectual senses dominate increasingly. The intellectual insight of man must run through several stages in order to reach the highest phase, a phase in which he sees all things in their *natural causality* and necessity. This deterministic line of reasoning led many of the nineteenth century to think further about the questions of culture and history. Besides the Frenchman Comte, we may mention the Englishman Herbert Spencer and his *System of Synthetic Philosophy* (1862ff.).

It was no accident that the idealistic views of history were, after a fruitful but short prosperity, surpassed by positivistic views. In the first place, man had taken his own insights and ideals as the standard for discovering meaning and observing direction and progress. But his own norms are also merely a moment in a progressing development. Thus, for present-day man, the source of knowledge and the norms for development must be sought from outside himself. Previously, these were sought in revelation. Now that man no longer considers himself in essence a child of God, he seeks the solutions of his existence elsewhere, namely in the events of nature of which he is a product. Idealism had not taken seriously this connection with the forces and laws of lower nature. It has now been discovered that by analogy the spiritual events, too, proceed from the natural; namely, within the framework of cause and effect.

This causal view of history could lead to the conclusion that history is a meaningless chaos, a sea without shore or form. The facts, however, show eloquently that the positivistic thinkers often tried to combine their causal-mechanistic explanation of the historical process, with an idea of goal-directedness. The foundation of this endeavour is the realization that whoever removes goal-directedness from this historical vision also removes the cultural strength from Europeans. Comte, the father of positivism, in the last phase of his life had already arrived at a kind of pantheistic religion in which 'humanity' takes the place vacated by God, in order to function as the meaning and goal of history. Something similar may be said of Spencer who saw peace and freedom of the modern state as the goal of previous development. Thus both combine their positivism with the idea of *evolution*. However, if we compare this expression and its contents with the high-pitched concept of humanity of romanticism and idealism, it will be found that a certain 'process of emaciation'[3] has taken place.

Nietzsche

Nietzsche was the one who recognized distinctly the Christian roots of evolution, and vigorously and completely rejected this dogma of his time. There is no progress, according to him, no efficiency, no 'higher moral world-order'. History is a meaningless play of the lust for power in which the weak man loses in order to make room for the Superman.

This latter seems yet another attempt to give meaning to history along the line of evolution. But this impression is shaken by Nietzsche's doctrine of the 'eternal return'. Considering the great, but not endless, variation of cause and effect, the same constellations will appear again and again for millions of years. It remains difficult to see how this view can be reconciled with the proclamation concerning the Superman and the lust for power. It has, therefore, always been considered a strange element in Nietzsche's system. This inconsistency is very significant, however. Nietzsche realized that in this doctrine he must from the beginning be aware of the current European sense of history, which was inspired by Christianity. He returned to the ancient concept of the cycle. Thus he has the animals say to Zarathustra,

> Everything goeth, everything returneth; eternally rolleth the wheel of existence. Everything dieth, everything blossometh forth again; eternally runneth on the year of existence. Everything breaketh, everything is integrated anew; eternally buildeth itself the same house of existence. All things separate, all things again greet one another; eternally true to itself remaineth the ring of existence. Every moment beginneth existence, around every 'Here' rolleth the ball 'There'. The middle is everywhere. Crooked is the path of eternity.[4]

The fact that life and history are meaningless was, for Nietzsche, a liberating confession.

Historicism

But the times in general shrank back from Nietzsche's radicalism. During contemporary and subsequent periods many significant attempts were made, especially by German thinkers, to free history from the grasp of naturalism. Most of the honour for this goes particularly to the neo-Kantian school of Baden (Windelband, Rickert) where history was seen in its own right, alongside naturalism, as the realization of values; it needs its own method of study. This effort contributed to the maintenance of the threatened independence of the so-called arts. But it has not been able to erect a barrier against the notion that history is without purpose. At the same time historical research gathered immense masses of material, which showed history to be an increasingly more detailed and extensive network of facts and connections. The attitude that would do justice to the peculiarity of history in its individuality, finality, and variegation, and which appreciates all cultural phenomena as phenomena in a historical process, we call *historicism*. This attitude was particularly widespread among Germans around, and shortly after, the turn of the century. Historicism has its roots in idealism. It rejects the thought of a mechanistic determinism of the events of history; it has, on the contrary, its eye on the surprising and creative in it. But it cannot as readily answer the question about the meaning of history as could the idealists of a century earlier. Are not all ideals, norms, and opinions themselves products of their own time? They are not above history, but they are results and elements of the historical process. Who can find certainty in this endless process? The great philosopher and theologian Ernst Troeltsch passionately sought for an answer to that question. Near the end of his life he included the results of this struggle in his large work, *Der Historismus und seine Probleme* (1922). In the spirit of Leibniz he seeks the solution in a pantheistic unity of finite and infinite spirit. The struggle in Troeltsch's thought between Christian and modern philosophy has not been resolved. His words at the end of his essays on 'Ethik und Geschichtsphilosophie' are typical:

> When it [history] gives a solution of its riddle and confusion, its contradictions and struggles, at all, the solution most probably does not lie within itself, but beyond it, in that unknown land to which so many of the historical rebellious minds point, but which itself never becomes visible.[5]

The Loss of the Sense of History

This tired scepticism was the result of more than a century

of deep and persistent thinking about the meaning of history. But they could not stay with this result. Along with the scepticism of historicism we note a *return to the pre-Christian, naturalistic, cyclical concept of history.* We have already seen how the mid-nineteenth-century thought of Nietzsche led in that direction. Before him, Schopenhauer had arrived at the old Indian concept of reality as a veil, or *maya.* The most characteristic thinker along this line after him was Oswald Spengler whose brilliant two-volume work, *Der Untergang des Abendlandes* (1918ff.),[6] had great influence after the First World War. According to Spengler every culture is a self-existent organism that follows the biological laws, living through a spring, summer, autumn, and winter, and then perishing irrevocably. Now the end of European culture approaches. And man is wise not to resist this lot, but to yield voluntarily to the demands of this last technological and dictatorial phase *(caesarism).* It is plain that we are dealing with a completely different sphere from that of historicism. But the return to pre-Christian concepts does not bring with it a return to the harmonious notion of life, in which life and death, rising and setting, are equally right. We cannot again become happy heathen. In Spengler and others (our choice of names must, of course, be limited), even in Nietzsche, we find homesickness, sadness, and resignation. This feeling of fatigue is common to both these views, and to historicism.

This matter was not confined to a small group of thinkers. They only voiced what was already astir in the subconscious spirit of Europe, and which became evident in the last, and more rapidly in this, century—that Europe is losing its sense of history. The idea that events are goal-directed, and that for this reason it is important to take part in history and to make sacrifices for the future, that idea made Europe great. Countless many have given themselves for the spreading of the gospel and humanitarianism, and for the sharing of civilization and progress, so that Europe became the leader of the world. But now we notice that we no longer have an answer to the questioning after purpose, and that we no longer even believe in a future worth living and dying for. It is still different with our younger sister America. There there is a stronger faith in a future to which they must give themselves. But what future? They think about a world in which the biological conditions of life have been strictly adhered to, and in which technology and hygiene deliver top performance. Here we clearly see the shoots of the earlier described 'process of emaciation'. Van der Leeuw puts it strikingly in his book (see note 3), when he says that the ideas which consecutively moved our civilization are: the Kingdom of God, Christianity, Man, progress, evolution, and technology.

> And the only thing that remains when the great process of emaciation ends, is the game. Everything follows predetermined rules, which in themselves might just as well have been different.[7]

Europe, however, is a few steps ahead of America in age, fatigue, and scepticism. Not so much because positivism and historicism pulled the rug from under our feet—although this is true—but two world wars accomplished much more, even with those who never read one of the hundreds of historical books dealing with past periods.

Wavering Counter-movements

Fortunately, we may also say that especially since the Second World War, some leading minds have been searching for new meaning in history. I trust to be not too arbitrary when I record three names in particular—those of the Germans Karl Jaspers and Rudolf Bultmann, and that of the Englishman Arnold Toynbee. We have already mentioned Jaspers' book *The Origin and Goal of History*. In spite of historicism he dares to draw large strokes. He places at about 1500 the first preambles of *Weltgeschichte*, which is now definitely ushered in by science and technology. Jaspers finds the meaning of history in the unity of mankind. But this is unattainable, and we cannot fill it with content because of the fundamental 'openness' of history. In this

'becoming', Jaspers does see that socialism and a certain
form of faith have been given a role to play. But the conclusion of it is that

> A perfect ideal unity can now also not be outlined clearly
> and without contradiction. This unity cannot become reality.
> Unity is much more of an infinite meeting place which is
> similar to origin and goal; it is the unity of transcendence.[8]

But now the question arises whether such a formal unity can
ever be the goal of our life and labour. The fact that Jaspers
will not and cannot say wherein and to what purpose this
unity is to be found proves that he cannot lead us out of the
crisis of historicism.

Although Bultmann, like Jaspers, stands in the existentialist tradition, he seeks a quite different road to overcome
historicism in his *History and Eschatology* (Edinburgh 1957).
Man is certainly led by his past, but real existence means
to be directed to a future. In this, man decides how far the
heritage of the past is useful for his future being. Thus the
relativity of the historical situation leads not to nihilism,
but has a positive sense when taken up in the freedom of
decision (a freedom that man can receive increasingly by
the road of forgiveness and faith). This movement towards
the future by decisions based on the past is what Bultmann
calls man's historicity. This existentialist interpretation
makes the question for a goal-directedness of history meaningless, since the question is in another sphere and cannot
be answered because we are neither above, nor at the end
of, history. The last paragraph of the Gifford Lectures
begins with the words:

> We started our lectures with the question of meaning in
> history, raised by the problem of historicism. We have seen
> that man cannot answer this question as the question of the
> meaning in history in its totality. For man does not stand out-
> side history. But now we can say: *the meaning of history lies
> always in the present,* and when the present is conceived as the
> eschatological present by Christian faith the meaning in
> history is realized.[9]

It is Bultmann's prerogative, of course, to give to the word 'history' an existential content. But he must not act as if by doing this he has given a real answer to the problems of historicism. He shifts the whole problem. By doing this he leaves the struggles of Troeltsch behind him and joins himself to the meaninglessness of history. In this way, and without difficulty, he gives up an essential notion of Christian faith which Troeltsch would happily have kept. The proverb 'the medicine is worse than the ailment' is applicable here.

It is still different with Toynbee in *A Study of History* (1934-39), and *Civilization on Trial* (1948). At first glance his thought seems to resemble Spengler. He shows us a series of self-sufficient cultures which have already seen their rise and fall. This is not, however, as in Spengler, the result of their tie to biological laws. Every culture is a *Gestalt* in which man struggles with the problems set before him. He can fail in this struggle; then the culture will be destroyed. He can also win and grow to great possibilities. Already twenty cultures have failed. The end of so-called Western civilization is not yet certain. But everything points to the fact that the cycle is the last secret of the process of history, This Toynbee does not want. Here begins what we may term his theology of history—that out of the suffering connected with the fall of a culture grows a deeper hunger for, and knowledge of, God. The cycle serves the evolution of religion and the enrichment of man's spiritual life.

This interesting view puts the meaning of history outside of itself, in the soul's individual relationship to God. However, Toynbee's statement about the evolution of religion is theologically and historically so contestable that it can hardly offer any inspiring strength. But more important, there is hardly any organic connection with his view of the historical process itself, which remains subject to the cycle.

None of these three views, although all search for new meaning, is able to break the ban which is rapidly setting itself upon the European culture; this is the notion that history is meaningless and purposeless. Once a person's eyes are accustomed to these things, he will discover the expressions everywhere: on the one hand expressions of great doubt, and on the other hand expressions of the passionate search for new meaning. Professor F. L. Polak's remarkable work, *De Toekomst is verleden Tijd* ('The Future is Past Tense', 1955), shows how deep this notion is, and with how much fear it has filled conscious minds. The writer is of the opinion that 'the rise and the fall of the image of the future precedes, and is coupled with, the rise and fall of the culture'.[10] Volume I deals with the classic views of the future under the heading, 'The Promised Land'; volume II, 'Breaking the Images of the Future', describes the weakening and undermining of the faith in the meaning of history (Polak calls it 'de-utopianizing') in the thinking of modern Europe. It seems quite plain how deep historicism has eaten into our sense of history.

> Our posterity already knocks at the gate; at the gate of the closed Kingdom of the Future. Shall we leave them to their own lot with an 'after us the flood', or shall we give them the answer of the first man to the first quickening call in the world—Here am I?[11]

It is typical that Polak's two-volume work gives a thorough diagnosis, without an equivalent therapy.[12] Obviously, one cannot put oneself to the task of building images of the future. This diagnostic consciousness remains sterile because it cannot break itself from the bounds of subjectivism. It is just not possible for us to create a sense of history. It is—or is not—given to us.

Marxism

However, over against this need and uncertainty in West-European thinking about the future and the meaning of history stands one powerful phenomenon of world dimension in which these questions are solved with great certainty and in a concrete manner—*Marxism*. This, too, is a product of Western Europe; and that from the nineteenth century.

Marx comes from the school of Hegel, but he moved on to a positivistic, or rather materialistic, line. We already observed that many positivists and naturalists continued to talk about 'progress', 'goal', and 'meaning'. This is also true in a large degree in Marx's thinking. This combination has become the great attraction of Marxism. The process of history is curbed and directed by 'scientifically fixed' laws of production-ratio and technology; laws that are formulated by historical materialism. With these laws as a basis, the future can be foretold with scientific certainty. The class struggle drives history on until capitalism collapses and the power over the means of production falls into the hands of the proletariat. Then ends the struggle between man and nature, man and man, individual and corporation. Injustice and crime will halt. Then man finally comes to himself. The Communist Manifesto enunciates the eschatology in the following classic words,

> In place of the old civil society with its classes and class struggles, there will be a community in which the free development of each is the condition for the free development of all.

Thus 'out of the night and need a new morning' of the classless society originates. Some have rightly pointed out the prophetic-messianic strain in the thought of the Protestant-educated Jew, Marx. Communism receives its astounding recruiting and driving power from the Judeo-Christian heritage, coupled with a naturalistic conformity to the law of the economic process. Is it not true that 'the naïve communist is a better believer in the future than the average Christian or even theologian'?[13]

The Threatening Alternative

These facts have led us into a dilemma of world proportion. On the one hand we find Western culture which, in the course of one and a half centuries, almost completely lost the notion of a meaning of history. On the other hand we find communism which is motivated by a solid and concrete conviction about the meaning of history. Western culture is weakened by the notion of meaninglessness; at the same time she wants with all her might to hold fast to the goods and values she had made her own during the centuries when faith in the future and goal-directedness of history still enabled her to do great things. Added to this is the fact that in the meantime the forces which were born out of this faith—desire to labour, impulse to develop, technical knowledge, care for the weak, democratic forms of government, etc.—have won the world, and have also liberated, or are liberating, the people of Asia and Africa from the cycle of their existence. These people now reach for the same forces to build their own future. But they are not able to develop these forces since they are not fed by a strong faith in the future of man and in the meaning of history. Will communism offer them this meaning? Then they must pay the price of bloody revolutions, fanaticism, dictatorship, and contempt for the individual. Will Europe and America offer them this meaning? But these often know no other meaning than that of materialistic and technological progress carried on by a vague humanitarianism or sceptical rationalism. Thus many nations must make the unfortunate choice between a wrong meaning or no meaning at all.

But we reject this threatening alternative with all our heart. It was the revelation of God that at one time helped us discover events as history. Only the road to that revelation can point out the way for us to the future. This book rests on the conviction that history has meaning, and that this can be found where Europe received it at one time—the revelation of God in Israel and in Jesus Christ. The following pages concern themselves with the description of, and reflection upon, the concept of history which is given with this revelation.

NOTES

[1] Karl Jaspers, *Vom Ursprung und Ziel der Geschichte* (1949, 1955), pp. 1, 5. English ed.: *The Origin and Goal of History*, New Haven, 1953.

[2] Guillaume van der Graft, 'Aangaande Abraham', *Vogels en Vissen*, Amsterdam, 1953, p. 51.

[3] This expression is borrowed from the important book by G. van der Leeuw, *Balans van het Christendom*, Amsterdam, 1940, pp. 28-40.

[4] *Thus Spake Zarathustra*, trs. T. Common, New York (The Modern Library), p. 223.

[5] In the posthumously published *Der Historismus und seine Überwindung*, Berlin, 1924, pp. 6of. This incorrect title is not Troeltsch's own.

[6] *The Decline of the West*, trs. C. F. Atkinson, London and New York, 1926-28.

[7] Van der Leeuw, p. 40; cf. pp. 28-40.

[8] Jaspers (1949 ed.), p. 333; (1955 ed.), p. 253. A little further one finds the words, 'the hidden kingdom of the candour of Being', 'invisible religion', and 'the Kingdom of the Spirit', which sound much like the quoted words of Troeltsch. Historicism has not been conquered.

[9] Rudolf Bultmann, *History and Eschatology: The Presence of Eternity*, Edinburgh and New York, 1957, pp. 154f. Note especially the entire last lecture.

[10] I, p. 27. In the original this is in italics.

[11] *Ibid*. II, p. 331.

[12] His clearest statement on this point is found in 'Responsibility for the Future and the Far-away', *Algemeen Nederlands Tijdschrift voor Wijsbegeerte en Psychologie* 49, 21 Jan. 1957, p. 81. Because it is important the statement is reproduced here: 'The split, now, is no longer between this and another, better society, but between the so-called idealists, looking *ahead*, and the so-called realists, looking *around*. The protagonists of the here-and-now seem to be gaining ground. Their eventual success might lead to a Pyrrhic victory. Because, if I may repeat, the final triumph will go to those people-of-two-worlds, who in deepest darkness keep their eyes on the radiant light of the City of Tomorrow. It will go to those who struggle along to the last breath in search of the Promised Land where their children's children may dwell in peace and happiness, at the glorious end of man's painful pilgrimage.'

[13] Eugen Rosenstock-Hüssy, *Heilkraft und Wahrheit*, Stuttgart, 1952, p. 38 (in italics).

2

HISTORY IN THE OLD TESTAMENT

The Old Testament writers find in the self-disclosure of God the factor in world events by which individual events are placed in a spiritual connection, and which makes events meaningful; i.e. only through it can a chaos of changing and hurrying events become comprehensible as real history. Under the impression of this divine experience they cannot describe world events in any other way than as historical succession in which everything is united under God's leading, and moves to a definite objective.

W. Eichrodt, 'Offenbarung und Geschichte im Alten Testament', *Theologisch Zeitschrift* IV, 1948, pp. 321f.

IN ISRAEL history was radically and permanently delivered from the law of nature, and therein history was discovered. Not in the sense that Israel found history in a unique act of thought; not even in the sense that she had discovered something that, although hidden, already existed. But the Israelites had come in contact with a God who changed events into history by his acts before their ears and eyes.

The Meaning of the Exodus and the Sense of History

The Old Testament is full of these acts. Yet it is clear that the origin of the sense of history is connected with one particular event which is indelibly imprinted into the spirit of Israel—the deliverance from Egypt in the miraculous crossing of the Red Sea. The witnesses in which this fundamental character of the intervention of God is set forth are numerous. Most telling is the fact that the remembrance of this intervention through the Passover festival formed the centre of Israel's worship. The Israelites expressed a confession of faith (according to von Rad a very old one) about the Exodus at the presentation of the firstborn (Deut. 26.5-9). They later dated their history from the Exodus (I Kings 6.1). All the institutions and ordinances of the life of Israel are posed against this background; the father must pass it on to his son (Deut. 6.20ff.).

In the mind of Israel this function of the Exodus was not yet necessarily of a history-making nature. We could presume that it functioned as a 'myth', an event of the dark past that laid the groundwork for Israel's existence, and for that reason must be continually remembered and celebrated. Israel's existence would then have been only a backward look based on repetition, and hence would still have been without history. One occasionally receives this impression, for instance, when one reads Deuteronomy or certain of the Psalms. But the impression is false. Many witnesses prove undeniably that the Exodus inaugurated a real history. God's deliverance was not a goal in itself, but was meant to be a leading into the promised land. Thus the forty years between the entry and the Exodus were goal-directed, and real history. But history did not stop in Canaan. History is there described as a movement toward a climax—the kingship of David. For it soon appears (see Judges) that the entry was not an actual fulfilment of history, partly because God's final goal is much broader, and partly because progress was hindered by Israel's unfaithfulness. For the same reason the climax under David and Solomon is not an end, either. The line of history declines to the exile. The major prophets and the later historical books see God continuing with his guidance and struggle. In the midst of all that is contrary to their expectation they wait for a new anointed one from the house of David, and for the Messianic Age in which God's leading of his people will reach its goal.

The Exodus is not a myth, but the beginning of history. It is praised as such in Psalms 78, 106, and 136, and in the moving confession of the Levites in Nehemiah 9. The remembrance of the Exodus is often found in accounts of the confession of sins (see II Kings 17.7, 36; Isa. 52.4-6; Jer.

2.6; 32.21ff.; Amos 2.10; 3.1f.; Micah 6.4; Pss. 78; 106).
It is man's fault that history has not yet reached its goal.
The unfaithfulness of man, and the faithfulness of God,
together keep history moving. The notion arose that God's
leading will only reach its goal when again a divine, miraculous intervention takes place, as before, when Israel went
through the Red Sea. The prophets often describe the
opening of the Messianic Age in terms of the deliverance
from Egypt, although they know that the coming deliverance
from anxiety and unfaithfulness will exceed the first (see
Isa. 4.5; 10.24-27; 11.16; 43.16ff.; 48.20f.; 52.12; Jer.
16.14f.; 23.7f.; 31.32; 32.39f.; Hos. 2.14; 12.10f.; Micah
7.15; Zech. 10.10-12).

Thus the real Exodus is still to come. However, this concerns not only Israel, but all nations. Israel's journey
through time has a world-wide purpose. Rest for Israel will
mean peace for all nations. The goal is not reached until all
nations halt their wars and go up to Zion to learn the law of
Yahweh (Isa. 2.1-5; Micah 4.1-5). God has set Israel apart
since the Exodus, in order that later she may become the
centre of a world in which all nations will belong to God
(Isa. 19.23-25). This mighty vision did not live in all
periods, and certainly not for all men; but it is the last unfolding of the sense of history that was set in motion with
the Exodus from Egypt.

The person and work of Jesus Christ cannot be understood
apart from this beginning of history with the Exodus.
Matthew especially, who writes for Jews, makes this plain.
Christ is called from Egypt (2.15); he goes through the
waters (3); he makes the journey through the desert (4); he
makes the covenant on the mountain (5); and when he dies,
he gives his life as the Passover Lamb whose blood saves not
only Israel, but now that the end time has arrived, also
means the exodus from the house of slavery for all nations.

Abraham

One may have wondered why we have related God's

39

history-making work so closely to the Exodus from Egypt, without having first mentioned the call of Abraham from Ur of the Chaldeans. Most of the historical and prophetic witnesses of the Old Testament point back to the Exodus, and very seldom in this connection to Abraham (if I have counted correctly only five times, all later passages: I Kings 18.36; II Kings 13.23; Ps. 105; Isa. 29.22; and Micah 7.20f.). It is different, however, in the history of the great historian-prophet whom we call the 'Yahwist'. He begins God's history-making actions with Abraham. This is connected with the function of Abraham in history as 'corporate personality'. Abraham is more than a historical figure: the history of his posterity is anticipated and included in his history. The exemplary, the prophetic, and the historical are so commingled in Genesis that it is unadvisable for us to seek the origin of Israel's sense of history here, when Israel herself directs us elsewhere. But precisely these prophetic and exemplary elements beginning at Genesis 12 are of extreme importance to us. Indeed, here is concentrated the whole meaning of the history of Israel. Abraham, and with him the whole nation, is called away from the naturalistic cycle of existence by which they lived in Mesopotamia. He starts on his way. He is a pilgrim oriented to a goal he does not reach. And that is not only *his* goal, for 'by you all the families of the earth shall bless themselves' (Gen. 12.3). Israel may often have known the temptation to break off the great journey temporarily; the witnesses whom we must thank for Genesis 12, many of the Psalms and books of prophecy knew that the nation was set upon a road that should end only when a refined Israel shall be the centre of a world of nations from which all blessings will flow and above which the Lord's glory would shine.

The Royal Psalms

It might seem that this way of thinking is concerned only with the people of Israel; and for many writers this will have been the case. But from the foregoing it is clear that all this, if reasoned through properly, has opened up the widest perspectives. These perspectives extend on the one hand to creation, and on the other hand to the *eschaton*—God's definitive triumph. This is particularly true of a number of Psalms which have great significance for our subject, the so-called Royal Psalms. Among these we include in a narrow sense those Psalms which praise God as the king of the world (47, 93, 96, 97, and 99), and in a broader sense many Psalms which, without this denomination, sing about God's reign over the world in all its extent through space and, especially, time (24, 46, 48, 75, 76, 92, 95, and 98). Since the related studies of the Norwegian scholar Mowinckel, it has become popular to explain these Psalms as arising from the cultus, and then especially to connect them with an annual Babylonian-oriented enthronement of divinity—in this case of Yahweh. However, the latter is subject to considerable dispute. Nothing is known in the Old Testament about an enthronement festival; to couple the Royal Psalms to this is like trying to explain the known by the unknown. It is possible to read into the Old Testament the function of these and many other Psalms in worship (see I Chron. 16; II Chron. 29 and 30). But the question remains whether these were composed for and because of worship, or whether they were used after they had originated elsewhere. Personally I believe the latter to be true of most of the Royal Psalms. Their origin is to be sought in concrete historical events. These were probably most often glorious victories over enemies or miraculous deliverances out of need, in which the poets saw the superior power of Yahweh against counterforces.

Psalm 93 suggests a good summary of the proclamation of the Royal Psalms. This Psalm begins like Psalms 97 and 99 with the expression *Yahweh malak*. The meaning of these words gives rise to deep-seated differences. We hold to the translation, 'The Lord is king', which is suggested by the sequence and the light accent on the verb which flows from the sequence. But the ancient Greek translation, the Septuagint, already translated it 'the Lord *has become* king', an opinion which we find also in the book of Revelation (see below). Some even translate it 'the Lord will become king'. This difference of opinion is not without meaning, for the Royal Psalms deal with a reign that includes past, present, and future. This is also the case in Psalm 93. Verse 1 looks for a special revelation of Yahweh's might in the present. The possibility of this depends on what is confessed in verse 2, 'Thy throne is established from of old.' God repeatedly intervenes triumphantly in order to reveal and confirm his kingship because he has executed his kingship over the earth since creation. He continues in history what he began in creation. Then he controlled the waters and the forces of chaos and gave them a place in his cosmos (see Gen. 1.2, 6f., 9f.). He maintains this work even when the 'waters' (vss. 2-4) raise themselves to disturb the order of creation. These 'waters' (the Israelites thought of the Nile, Tigris, and Euphrates) are here the names of the world powers which threaten Yahweh's people and work. But he does not leave undone what his hand began. God confirms his act of creation in the fact that these threatening powers are continually subdued. The decrees concerning his kingship prove themselves to be 'very sure' (vs. 5a). The poet sees the temple in its holiness and its inviolability as a sacramental indication of the fact that the forces of chaos cannot disturb this work (vs. 5b). He knows that for this reason he can look to the future with confidence. The certainty that this superior power of God cannot come to an end is sounded in the words, 'for evermore'. When we compare this song with other Royal Psalms such as 96 and 98, and when we compare their closing words, there is reason to read more into the words, 'for evermore', namely, a view to the future, final revelation of God's reign as king, in which he as ruler will subjugate the proud adversary for ever. It is easily understood that from this standpoint some might want to translate *Yahweh malak* as 'the Lord will become king'. If we consider the Royal Psalms as a group it is clear that God's kingship is active in creation, in history, and in consummation. That which in creation was only a beginning will later be completely realized through the pains of history.

This view has a special interpretation in Psalm 75, which in the broader sense may be considered of this same group. In this Psalm the poet speaks with God. As is so often true of the Psalms of Asaph, we find here a man in temptation. He sees that the proud triumph and that the godly are defeated. He asks how this can be possible. God himself gives him the insight and the perspective by which he can persevere in the face of this temptation (vss. 2 and 3). This counsel of God directs him to the future (vs. 2), and to creation (vs. 3), in which the last reverence clearly serves as the foundation of the first,

> At the set time which I appoint
> I will judge with equity.
> When the earth totters, and all its inhabitants,
> it is I who keep steady its pillars.

The latter took place in creation. Its order can be threatened, but it cannot be destroyed. The forces of Chaos may gain the upper hand for a time, but this happens by virtue of God's patience, and in time they will make room for his reign which will set everything right (see vss. 7f.). It is useless to ask here whether the Psalmist thought of a 'historical' or an 'eschatological' event. Here, as elsewhere in the Psalms, the perspectives are commingled. Every historical victory of Yahweh over the adversary is on the one hand a confirmation of his act of creation, and on the other hand a pledge of his coming, final blessing. History is the road by which the king strives 'conquering and to conquer' (Rev. 6.2) from creation to consummation.

This quotation from the book of Revelation is not here by accident. The witness of the Royal Psalms concerning history resounds clearly in the New Testament proclamation. At times the theme of the Royal Psalms is almost literally, expressly, and consciously copied in Revelation. The *Yahweh malak* is heard in the heavenly songs of praise which accompany God's struggle in history. 'The kingdom of the world has become the kingdom of our Lord and of his Christ, and he shall reign for ever and ever' (Rev. 11.15; see also 11.17f.; 12.10, and 19.6). The Royal Psalms show us the broad perspectives in which life from the Exodus was understood, or at least came to be understood as time went on. The election and deliverance of Israel, and God's guiding and teaching presence through the wilderness, Canaan, and the exile, form the central events of salvation in which the secret of his concern with the whole world is accepted and understood. God's concern for Israel is an amazing deviation from the normal cycle of existence. But, as the Royal Psalms proclaim, this concern has become the centre which illuminates the cycle, which now appears to be not a cycle at all, but goal-directed history.

The Prophets

The description of the proclamation of the Royal Psalms has led us to the related witness of the prophets. History is *the* central theme with them. This, of course, is to express it too academically. Their theme is God in relationship with Israel and the world; a relationship of judgment and grace both today, tomorrow, and in the last days. They confess and proclaim Yahweh as the God of history. The emphases, however, are different from those in the Royal Psalms. At any rate, the proclamation of the prophets, taken as a whole, exceeds that of the Royal Psalms in two points.

In the first place, the opposing forces are seen not only as adversaries, but even more as instruments of God's rule. This is confessed very strongly concerning Assyria in Isaiah 10. The knowledge that God struggles in history with his adversaries did not lead Israel to dualism, as was the case with Zarathustra. God is still sovereign over his own struggles. He even uses the adversaries and executes his judgments through them in order to chastise or glorify Israel and the nations. Isaiah saw Assyria used this way, as Ezekiel and Jeremiah saw Babylon. Thus, the locusts of

Joel 1 and 2 are signs of God's judgments, and the omen of the coming, final judgment.

In the second place, Israel, more strongly than before, is counted among the powers which hinder the unfolding of God's reign. In this respect, Isaiah is nearest the Royal Psalms. The sanctuary and the nation are for him unassailable as tokens of God's insuperable faithfulness. This is no longer true in Ezekiel and Jeremiah. God rejects his people and his sanctuary (Jer. 7.1-15; Ezek. 9f.). But the fall of Israel and the destruction of the temple do not mean victory for the adversaries, but rather chastening by God's loving wrath, aided by the adversaries. One can see how this second view is connected with the first. God's struggle in history loses all appearance of nationalistic narrowness. The One who temporarily rejects Israel and chooses Cyrus as his instrument, is at the same time the God who remains veiled. And yet, in all this he is the Redeemer whose love will triumph (Isa. 45.15). This is seen best in Deutero-Isaiah.

We shall choose a few passages from the prophetic writings which deserve our particular attention in connection with this if we wish to examine the subject a little closer; these include the so-called apocalypse of Isaiah (24-27), the vision of the future in Ezekiel (36-39), Deutero-Zechariah, and Daniel 7. These contain curious, concrete expressions of the sense of history which led to the apocalyptic era. These are of real significance if we are to understand the minds of Jesus and the apostles when they, in this respect too, lived 'from the Scriptures'.

The Apocalypse of Isaiah

First the apocalypse of Isaiah. Mentioning it first does not mean that it is the oldest of the four witnesses; this is possible but not at all certain. Many authors, including Beek, defend the opinion that this passage comes from the pen of Isaiah, about 750 BC and that it was written after the earthquake which destroyed the city of Moab, in order to induce the inhabitants to seek refuge in Jerusalem.[1] On the other hand, there is an opinion held by many that it is dated shortly before the close of the canon (*c.* 270 BC) and that if it concerns Moab (which is disputed) it points to the conquest of the area by the Nabateans in the first part of the third century.[2] The date is of little importance to our study (for other subjects, especially the resurrection of the dead, it is extremely valuable) since we deal here with the view of history it contains. It deals with a deep humiliation of the city and country of Moab. The prophet sees in this the triumph of God's judgment over his enemies and grace for his people. At the same time he already sees in this historical event the beginning of the final judgment and the last kingdom. The prophet views the fall of Moab as the dawning of the fall of the world, while the delivered Zion becomes the place where sorrow and death are banished, and the feast is prepared for all nations.

The combination of these perspectives and the penetration of events to the great End are essential to the prophetic experience of history.

> The writer places here an event which takes place within the framework of history—the fall of Moab—into the eschatological end time, and sees the political enemy, Moab, changed into an eschatological enemy of the end time, even an enemy in the future Kingdom of God.[3]

This passage played an important role in the eschatology of the primitive Christian Church; quotations would include Matt. 21.42; I Cor. 15.54; Rev. 20 and 21.

Ezekiel 36-39

We find the same insight in Ezekiel's vision of the future of the world and Israel, but with a different slant. Ezekiel lived during the exile. While Jeremiah (and also, to some extent, Deutero-Isaiah) united the return from the exile with the expected day of salvation, Ezekiel looked further into the future. The coming return was also eschatological for him, as are all of God's dealings with Israel; his judgment and grace are even now active here. But this does not prevent him from working out his own opinion about the historical succession of events. The salvation of God in the return from Babylon is sung in chapter 36. The expectation that the kingdom of the ten tribes and of the two tribes will be united under a descendant from the house of David is connected with this in 37.15ff. At the same time the famous vision of the valley of the dry bones (37.1-14) refers to the fact that the return in itself still has no meaning without the quickening Spirit of Israel's God. But after the return, the Spirit will be poured out upon the nation. This will still not be the consummation, however. All this is not God's last, but his next-to-last word. After this a terrible power will raise itself against God and his people. It is 'Gog, of the land of Magog, the chief prince of Meshech and Tubal' (38.2). The name Magog is present in the so-called table of nations (Gen. 10.2), together with those of other nations which are thought to be in the vicinity of the Caucasus and Caspian Sea. For Ezekiel the name had the terrible sound of 'the far north' of the barbarians, the powers of political chaos. With this country is connected the name of a ruler, Gog. Attempts to prove that he was a historical figure (e.g. Gyges) have been inconclusive. It is more probable that the name is a derivative of Magog; a duplication with an ominous sound. Gog is the mysterious pseudonym of the yet unknown adversary who is seen to appear by Ezekiel after the return from the exile. His appearance is partly explained in historical terms. But the figure is broadened. Gog is the greatest, last adversary summoned by God in order to demonstrate his divine, superior power. Gog is an eschatological entity. The whole cosmos is involved in battle against him (38.20). Victory over him will mean the unshakable reign of God. In New Testament terms, Gog is the antichrist; the last and most complete expression of the waters which, according to Psalm 93, raise their roar against the kingship of Yahweh. The knowledge that in every struggle between Yahweh and his adversaries the end, the *eschaton*, is at stake, was coupled in Ezekiel and others (see below on Daniel; perhaps also the writer of the Isaiah apocalypse with his concept of Moab?) with the conviction that there is still to be a last struggle which will exceed all others and which will decide the battle forever. Beek dares to go one step further by suggesting that the return of Israel and the outpouring of the Spirit (Ezek. 37) is the next to the highest expression of God's superior might. He views it as a 'kingdom-between', and calls Ezekiel the creator of the idea of the millennial kingdom.[4] The Revelation of John, at any rate, understood Ezekiel 37f. this way. The roots of the millennial kingdom of Revelation 20 are not in the postcanonical Jewish apocalypses, but in Ezekiel 37 and 38! The fact that this kingdom ends with the rise of Gog and Magog, and that their fall is described by quotations from Ezekiel 38, removes all doubt. We shall come back to this theme when we discuss the millennial kingdom. Here we have tried to point out how Ezekiel gave a few new twists to the prophetic vision of history; or better, how he drew further consequences from this vision.

Deutero-Zechariah

In the second part of Zechariah (9-14) the figure of the historical-eschatological future is still more variegated. This passage is often called Deutero-Zechariah because it deals with another theme than the first half of the book and is, therefore, often ascribed to another prophet who lived either after Zechariah or before the exile. The latter is improbable. The exile and diaspora are taken for granted (e.g. 10.9-10), and the deliberately mysterious character of the passage is already a transition to the apocalyptic. In my opinion there are no compelling reasons for not assigning the passage to Zechariah. But the question of date, for our purpose, is not of decisive importance. The uncertainty about the date is of less concern than uncertainty about its meaning. The composition is uncertain, the text is at times corrupt, and it is often deliberately enigmatic. For all these reasons it is not advisable for laymen to concern themselves with details. The main point, however, is very clear. These prophecies have a concrete, historical origin in the corruption of Judah's leaders (the 'shepherds' of 10 and 11), and in the pagan practices of idolatry and false prophecy (10.2; 13.1-6). The revelation of God's power in the return from Babylon is past. The Jews experience what Ezekiel had foreseen; the Kingdom of God did not come in this way. The struggle between Yahweh and his adversaries continues. A new, great, and decisive battle is in prospect. This battle will be against the enemies which in the near future will threaten Israel. Attention is directed particularly to Egypt, Assyria, Persia, and Greece. They will march against Jerusalem and almost subjugate it. Israel's unfaithfulness is the reason why it goes this far. She can function as the centre of a world of nations only after a radical purification. A mysterious shepherd will be raised up in Judah who will take up the cause of the oppressed nation on behalf of God. But his work is ignored, and for that reason his labour will bring judgment to Israel (11.4-17). This person is probably the same as the one who will be pierced through (12.10-14). The moment will arrive when Israel will realize how she has sinned against God. God even says in 12.10, 'they shall look upon me whom they have pierced' (KJV).[5] They will raise a lamentation for the dead, and God will deliver the distressed city through his appearance on the Mount of Olives (14.1-7). The divided nation of Israel will then be reunited, the defeated nations will repent. Jerusalem will become the cultic world-centre, and the time of the great works of the Spirit has arrived in which the division between holy and profane will disappear (14.8-21). Thus the kingdom of peace opens. A king will reign in Zion who will remove the horses of war and ride upon a donkey (9.9f.). He will come from a simple folk out of a group of oppressed, god-fearing people. He is called a 'redeemed one'. Is he the revived shepherd? It is possible that Zechariah has in mind the suffering servant of Isaiah 53 in this expression of humility and glorification.

These mysterious chapters have much to say to us. We

have here the same image of a final alliance of adversaries before the completion, as was found in Ezekiel. But there are new twists. Israel herself will belong with the adversaries. In the *Gestalt* of the pierced shepherd the work of God will seem to have reverted to nothing. Broad roads of sorrow and purification lie ahead for the nation. Due to the sin of the world, particularly the sin of his own people, God's road to the kingdom follows a bitter detour.

The pages of the New Testament are full of allusions to this detour. These chapters have been of stupendous significance for Jesus' sense of messiahship and Passion, as well as for the christological concepts of the New Testament writers. The Prince of peace rides a donkey (compare Zech. 9.9 with Matt. 21.5 and John 12.15), and will return in that same manner (Matt. 23.39). The shepherd is slain and the sheep are scattered (compare Zech. 13.7 with Matt. 26.31 and Mark 14.27). He is valued at only thirty pieces of silver (compare Zech. 11.12f. with Matt. 26.15; 27.9). Soon they will realize who it was whom they pierced, and all the races of the earth will mourn for him (compare Zech. 12.10 with John 19.37 and Rev. 1.7). When Jesus wanted to discuss the coming Kingdom he went to the Mount of Olives (Matt. 24.3; Mark 13.3); he bids farewell on this mountain and the angels proclaim that he will return in the same manner (Acts 1.11). The significance of this mountain in the expectation of Jesus and his followers must have been derived from Zech. 14.4. The book of Revelation contains a number of quotations and allusions which must have been drawn from the description of the kingdom of peace in Zechariah 14 (compare Rev. 11.15; 21.25; 22.1, 3, 5 with Zech. 14.7, 8, 9, and 11).

Daniel 7

In conclusion, we shall discuss Daniel 7 with special emphasis. The entire second part of Daniel (7-12) is of importance for our study; but here we are not able to go into the numerous exegetical details. This is not necessary, however, since Daniel 7 contains the book's whole vision of history; and this chapter, more than the following, has made its influence felt in the apocalypses, the New Testament, and the Christian Church.

The second half of Daniel is the first writing we can include in the group of Jewish apocalypses. It is generally agreed that the book was written about 165 BC. The eschatological visions are closely connected with historical events. Israel is oppressed by the kingdoms of the world. It is now the cruel, Assyrian ruler Antiochus IV Epiphanes, who excludes nothing and no one from his plan to Hellenize the Jews, and to draw them away from their God. It has been suggested that Daniel received the well-known vision of the four beasts in a dream. The interpreters have often concentrated their attention upon the one question of what political powers these are supposed to be. Are they kingdoms or kings? Are they thought to be successive or simultaneous? What does Daniel really have in mind? These questions are not important for our purpose. Generally it is of little value to ask these questions of apocalyptic literature, since in the struggle between God and the adversaries the same constellations reappear which are indicated by the ancient names ('Gog', 'beasts', and 'Babylon'). One day these powers will display the extreme of their blasphemous might. These eschatological powers are already prefigured in various historical nations. Daniel is not primarily concerned with who the four beasts are (it is significant that apocalypses never name contemporary individuals), but he is concerned to gain insight into history by which the faithful can see these powers in the right perspective and find courage to face their struggle and suffering.

Daniel sees a sea stirred up by the winds, as a figure of formless and chaotic world events. Four alliances rise from the sea. They are beasts. They are strange, terrifying, and mighty. They lack humanity. They are subhuman, 'beastly'. A small horn develops on the head of the fourth beast which actually supersedes the pride and power of the other alliances. It dares to blaspheme God and go to battle against his

people. But his last purposes are not realized. Merely three
and a half seasons are allotted to him, half of the perfect
period of seven seasons (vs. 25). The celestial judgment
intervenes. The fourth beast is killed, and the life span of
the other three is limited. Power on earth is then taken over
by 'one like a son of man', who is taken (from the earth) on
the clouds before the throne of God. World events change
precisely at the critical moment. The beasts have ruled until
now. The new ruler, however, is like a son of man. God's
reign finally brings real humanity.

Who is this one who is like a son of man (i.e. like a man)?
This expression in Daniel is not a title. It is one of these
vague and mysterious descriptions which often occur in the
apocalypses. The explanation says that the person in the
vision (the antagonist of the beast) signifies a community;
namely, the 'people of the saints of the Most High' (vs. 27)
who are oppressed by the horn of the fourth beast. It seems
to be an alliance like that of the kingdoms of the beasts
(vs. 23). It is not necessary, as many interpreters have done,
to separate the vision as an earlier element from the interpretation, which was added later. The figure of the son of
man is clearly meant to be metaphorical. History will lead to
the victory of God over a blasphemous adversary, after
which the eternal kingdom will be governed by the oppressed faithful of Israel.

We shall return to this passage in the next chapter; for
this vision continued to influence the faith and thought of
Israel even after Antiochus IV Epiphanes was long for-
gotten. Jesus, who called himself the Son of Man, was influenced by this vision.

Some Conclusions

1. If we compare the witness of the Royal Psalms with
that of Daniel 7, we find that, despite the historical gulf of
several centuries, *the fundamental concept was essentially the
same.* This is true even of the witnesses we have discussed,
and which fall between the two. What takes place in the

events of man is no illusion, cycle, or formless ocean, but the terrain on which God executes his battle against the adversaries. The outcome of the battle is certain. It is anchored in creation. Every indication of God's superior power is also an indication of the coming Kingdom. Each indication may be the institution of that Kingdom. If this is not the case, the expectation continues unperturbed to look for new indications.

2. While in the older witnesses the sense of history is primarily a backward glance, and while it existed in God's history-making act of the Exodus, *the emphasis was later shifted* increasingly to the present (the Royal Psalms), to the near future (the earlier prophets), and even to an indefinite future (after the exile). At this point we may speak of a growth in the sense of history. The apostasy of their own people, and the threats from without, led the witnesses to view the struggle as not yet completed. Indeed, long roads and detours were still ahead.

3. The struggle repeats itself on these roads again and again, in similar forms. In later ages the struggles are described in terms of earlier centuries. But there is not only repetition. The last struggle will contain a tremendous *increase* in battle. The adversaries will stake everything on this last stand, but God's victory will overcome even that. The adversaries will exhaust themselves, and the result will be the Lord's complete kingship over his people, and over all nations.

4. In light of this, the question must be answered whether Israel's expectation is 'on this side' (*diesseitig*), or 'on the other side' (*jenseitig*). It is often said that the earlier prophets saw the 'kingdom' as a reality on earth and in history, and that in later centuries, especially in apocalyptic literature, the kingdom was seen in a new dispensation which can become reality only by a break with the present age. This difference is undeniable. It is connected with the growth of the sense of history discussed above. For that reason the difference is not a contradiction. The kingdom of peace in Isaiah 11 is quite different from the situation in Isaiah's

own time. On the other hand, the kingship of Daniel 7, which belongs to the people of the Most High, will take place on the same earth on which the beast ruled. To talk here about 'two types of eschatology' is a mere speculation. Connected with this is the fact that we do not need Zarathustra's religion to explain the differences between the early and later witnesses of the Old Testament. It is not known to what extent this influenced Israel during the Persian occupation. We do not know Israel's positive and negative reactions to it. The fundamentals of Parsiism or dualism (the god of light against the god of darkness) are irreconcilably foreign to Israel's faith, according to which the adversaries too are in God's hand and plan. If particular notions of Zarathustra's religion (e.g. dualism of present and future, resurrection, and judgment) had any influence on later prophets and apocalypses, they only awakened what was already present below the surface. For the development of the sense of history in the Old Testament is a steady, organic flow without deviations.

5. It follows that we must be critical about the popular contradiction between prophecy and apocalyptic. It is an impossible task to separate the two, in definition. One could say that apocalypses prefer to deal with detailed predictions of the future, with numbers, and seasons. But predictions are also numerous in the earlier prophets, and the use of numbers and seasons is also present in other types of literature of the Old Testament (see Gen. 15.13f.). The differences are no more than obvious differences of emphasis. Perhaps it is more important to note that the prophets speak to the unfaithful nation, while the apocalypses address themselves to the faithful remnant. It might be said, then, that the first address themselves more to unbelievers and call for repentance, while the latter are esoteric and bring comfort.[6] There was always the danger for apocalypses to become the hobby of the sects. This is exactly what has happened. But this fact does not tell against apocalypses any more than the presence of false prophets tells against prophecy. The progress we have described from the Royal Psalms to

Daniel 7 shows variation and expansion, but not deviation. Whoever accepts the prophetic view of history cannot reject Daniel 7 and Revelation as being of a different spirit. If we want to overcome sectarianism, we must first overcome our fear of apocalypses which still haunts many circles in the Christian Church.

6. It will be clear from the preceding that we cannot understand the proclamation of the New Testament if we refuse to listen to the Old Testament witnesses discussed in this chapter. They apparently played an important role in the life of Jesus, and in the hearts and minds of the apostles; a much larger role than we dare to suppose. It is not possible to accept the New Testament proclamation concerning the relationship of God and history without accepting in principle the related witness of the prophets and apocalypses. To a certain degree this observation holds also for the non-canonical apocalyptic literature of the inter-testamental period. It contributed to the atmosphere in which Jesus and his apostles lived and to their attention to the more apocalyptic parts of the Old Testament.

NOTES

[1] M. A. Beek, *Inleiding in de Joodse Apocalyptiek van het Oud- en Nieuw-Testamentisch Tijdvak*, Haarlem, 1950, vol. II, §2.

[2] E. S. Mulder, *Die Teologie van die Jesaja-Apokalypse*, Groningen, 1954, p. 93. For a survey of the various opinions see the third chapter, *passim*.

[3] *Ibid.*

[4] Beek, *op. cit.*, vol. II, §4.

[5] This is the proper translation (*elai* means 'to me'), which is also found in the Septuagint. In this way only does a comparison with the executed deity, Hadad-Rimmon, make sense. Many exegetes and translators shy away from this unusually bold identification of God and a man, and follow several old manuscripts with read *elaw* ('to him') which is more easily connected with the use of the third person following it.

[6] Martin Buber, *Sehertum, Anfang und Ende*, 1955, pp. 49-74. Buber considers this primarily a qualitative difference. The prophet sees the possibility to change history, and, therefore, calls for a reversal. The apocalyptists wait for a reversal by God. The Christian who views man

as other than a partner in the covenant, will not reject apocalypses because of this difference; but he will see this difference as one of situation rather than attitude of faith. Von Rad (*Theology of the Old Testament*, vol. II, §I) also rejects apocalyptic—as timeless, deterministic, pessimistic, etc. He sees no relation with the prophets, only with Wisdom literature.

3

JESUS CHRIST THE END OF HISTORY

Jesus said: 'The time is fulfilled, and the kingdom of God is at
hand.' 'But if it is by the Spirit of God that I cast out demons, then
the kingdom of God has come upon you.'
Mark 1.15; Matt. 12.28.

Jesus as the 'Remnant'

JESUS LIVED entirely by and from the Old Testament. The
consciousness of his unique calling was gained from his involvement with the Father in a way that we cannot understand. But his involvement with the Old Testament as the
revelation of the Father had a definite influence on that
impenetrable event. In many ways that influence is also
veiled from observation. Yet, we have good reasons to suppose that Jesus found his place and task as Messiah particularly in two chapters—Isaiah 53 and Daniel 7. In the first,
he saw his humiliation foretold: a road of contempt and
suffering, and a substitutionary death. In the second, he
read the glorious crowning of this road: the receiving of
power over all the kingdoms of the world from the hand of
God. He knew that he was to be the Suffering Servant and
the Son of Man united in one. It is possible that Deutero-
Isaiah originally meant the Suffering Servant to be a group,
a society; the holy, substitutionary remnant of the people.
We noted above that a plural was intended, in any case,
with the Son of Man, 'the people of the saints of the Most
High'. The prophets have repeatedly expressed their trust
in the faithful remnant which, as a substitute, will realize
God's intentions for Israel. Jesus knew that he alone was

57

the remnant. He would not remain alone, but would bear fruit and make many righteous only when he alone showed trust, and took the suffering upon himself. The work of Jesus' Messianic realization consisted of making both the above-mentioned passages relevant to his own person and work.

Relating these passages to one individual instead of to a collection of persons was not unique to Jesus. We know that the Son of Man in Daniel 7 was considered as an individual by the apocryphal writing of Enoch which was largely composed during the second century BC, probably shortly after Daniel. It was also so considered by the apocryphal IV Ezra (last part of the first century AD). It is not difficult to explain this. Were not the beasts of Daniel 7 also called kings (vs. 17) who ruled kingdoms (vs. 23)? The collection is united in an individual. In Judaism the boundaries between group and representative run together. It is easy, then, to accept the Son of Man described as an individual, in this way. The ancient synagogue, too, saw the Son of Man as an individual.

Jesus, Daniel, and Enoch

These and other considerations led, among several others, the famed historian of religion, Rudolf Otto,[1] to the position that Jesus took his understanding as the Son of Man not (at least not primarily) from Daniel, but from Enoch. He appeals especially to Enoch 71.14, in which the Ancient of Days, surrounded by his angels, approaches Enoch and greets him with the words, 'This is the Son of Man.' Here Enoch is simultaneously exalted and enthroned as the Son of Man. Otto finds here an explanation of the fact that Jesus wanted to keep his Messiahship secret, and that he speaks about the Son of Man in the third person. Jesus expected that God would raise him as the Son of Man in the approaching consummation in the same manner as it was foretold in the book of Enoch.

At first glance this hypothesis is attractive, but after closer examination it calls for reconsideration. We have no evidence that Jesus was acquainted with the book of Enoch, and we do not find any trace of Jesus' identification with Enoch. According to the quotations, Jesus' use of the name 'Son of Man' goes back to Daniel. We do not need a hypothesis like Otto's since the New Testament itself points to Daniel 7 as the origin of the title 'Son of Man'. Besides, the spirit of the Gospels differs greatly from that of the book of Enoch, precisely because of the unity between humiliation and exaltation, between Suffering Servant and Son of Man in Jesus of Nazareth. For all these reasons, a knowledge of the book of Enoch does not add to the understanding of Jesus' selfunderstanding and preaching. We seek the key (at least one important key) where Jesus himself directs us—in Daniel 7.

> Jesus already had an idea of the Son of Man that comprised a whole theology of history in itself. In calling himself the Son of Man Jesus had already taken the decisive step in claiming cosmic history as his own.[2]

This is correct. We must not suppose, as is often done consciously as well as unconsciously, that Jesus took only the name from Daniel 7, coupled with a certain idea of exaltation. Jesus lived from the vision and proclamation of this chapter. The knowledge that he was the Son of Man meant to him the knowledge that he had a function in the great drama of history pictured by Daniel. He knew that the beasts had arrived at their greatest, blasphemous strength. He also knew that God's mighty intervention was at hand, and that he himself had been appointed to take over the government of the world. He expressed this publicly at the most critical moment of his life, during the proceedings of the Jewish court (Mark 14.62ff.). He was condemned to death because of this confession. More than once a Jew had considered himself to be the Messiah. This was in itself no reason to be accused as a blasphemer since in Jewish tradition the Messiah was often seen as a mere man (Acts 5.36f.). But it was quite different when someone dared to identify himself with the celestial figure of the Son of Man who stands in a unique relationship with the Almighty and the clouds of heaven. That was blasphemy, and for that reason Jesus was crucified.

'You will see the Son of man seated at the right hand of Power, and coming on the clouds of heaven.' Matthew adds the phrase, 'from now on' (26.64; 'hereafter' in RSV), and Luke does the same (22.69), although the words in Greek are somewhat different. This addition makes the meaning still plainer. Jesus knew that he had come to bring the close of history. Man's evil and the superhuman adversaries come to their zenith, and surround him as though they are messengers from God. He knows that he has come to lead the world to its crisis, but also to overcome that crisis.

The Great Division at Jesus

The next chapter will discuss a more far reaching notion about Jesus' confession before the Sanhedrin, but here we are concerned only with the life and death of Jesus in the light of this confession. He saw himself as the one through whom and around whom the historical crisis was to take place. The Royal Psalms had sung about this crisis. Even now the waters roar, and now Yahweh, represented in Jesus, will prove to be mightier than the sound of many waters. In the Royal Psalms there is no certainty that this is the decisive battle, but it is a certainty with the crisis released by Jesus. The Messianic Age the prophets looked forward to has now arrived. The adversaries gather all their might, but they move toward complete destruction. A very strange atmosphere is presented by the Gospel stories about Jesus' earthly life: an atmosphere of fearful anguish, and at the same time of joy and freedom. In Jesus, history is finally reduced to its hitherto mysterious, fundamental forces. The writer of the Gospel of John understood this especially, but the synoptic Gospels also repeatedly witness to this fact. The great division takes place around Jesus.

In their meeting with Jesus we see men fall on one side or

the other—the rich young ruler, the woman of Samaria, Nicodemus, the Pharisees, and the disciples—for Jesus 'is set for the fall and rising of many in Israel' (Luke 2.34). He did not come to bring peace, but a sword. He casts fire upon the earth and causes a division between one man and another and he then rightly asked, 'Why do you not know how to interpret the present time?' (Luke 12.49-56). 'For judgment I came into the world, that those who do not see may see, and that those who see may become blind' (John 9.39). Neutrality and indifference must clear the field. Only the 'pro' and 'con' for Jesus remain. The official religion is 'con'. More and more Jesus comes to stand alone. The adversaries will summon together all their power. There can be no other way, for by his appearance and work Jesus called them to life. The activities of the demons around Jesus must also be viewed in this light. The manner in which they enslaved men during the life of Jesus is, for those who recognize the time, the omen that the last round has started. The great hour in which the power of darkness triumphs over the work of God now breaks over the whole world (Luke 22.53; Matt. 26.45; John 7.30; 8.20).

It is, at the same time, the hour of the enthronement of the Son of Man (John 13.1). The Old Testament belief that the power of darkness will meet its final hour only because of the superior power of God, remains unbroken (John 19.11). For that reason the anguish is coupled with a deep joy. 'I saw Satan fall like lightning from heaven' (Luke 10.18). The demons tremble before Jesus, 'Have you come here to torment us before the time?' (Matt. 8.29). Jesus expels the demons, and explains the meaning of this in the following words, 'But if it is by the finger of God that I cast out demons, then the kingdom of God has come upon you' (Luke 11.20; Matt. 12.28). The less frequently used verb *phthano* (lit. 'precede') is used here for 'has come upon you', which appears also in the well-known translation of Dan. 7.22 by Theodotion. It is possible that this expression of Jesus contains an allusion to the vision of the Son of Man.

The entire Gospel narrative deals with struggle and victory. We only point to the mysterious words of Matt. 11.12, and compare them with Luke 16.16. The rendering[3] of the Revised Standard Version footnote reads, 'From the days of John the Baptist until now the kingdom of heaven has been coming violently, and men of violence take it by force.' The translation, 'the kingdom of God has been coming violently', is less probable when we consider the words that follow it, and the fact that the arrest of John the Baptist gave rise to these words, while the context deals with the opposition to John and Jesus. The verb can also be translated in a passive voice, 'the kingdom of heaven has suffered violence'. This agrees much better with the context.[4] It then means the enemy who is called up by the Kingdom. The words of Luke 16.16 are somewhat similar, 'The law and the prophets were until John; since then the good news of the kingdom of God is preached, and everyone enters it violently.' The context here is entirely different. In so far as there is a question of context, the good news of the gospel stands here in opposition to pharisaism. The daring verb *biazetai* from Matthew 11 is here replaced by *euangelizetai*. *Biazetai* does appear but is moved to the second part of the text where it is translated as 'enters violently'. It is obvious that both texts come from the same words of Jesus, but it is not possible to ascertain which of the two is the original. It is more important to note that the original was understood in such contradictory ways. This double meaning is certainly in agreement with Jesus' view of the Kingdom. The Kingdom was proclaimed as good news (*euangelizetai*) in order that everyone may enter it violently; and it suffers violence (*biazetai*) because men of violence reach for it. This is the situation in the eschatological cycle of history.

> The pursuit of the enemy as well as the approach to man, for which the old boundaries are no longer valid, are both, if viewed from their content, negative and positive aspects of the only reality; so that the decisive turning point, which at the same time must become a battle, has stormily entered in power.[5]

The Cross and Resurrection as the End of History

If the life of Jesus must be seen in this light, it must be equally true of the death which he consciously accepted as the necessary way to victory. We learned from the prophets that the 'Day of the Lord' arrives with much struggle and judgment. Jesus knew that the great Messianic woes would have to precede his triumph. Apart from the question whether Jesus and the Gospel writers gave a broader interpretation to the concept of the Messianic woes (this was certainly the case as will be seen in the next chapter), it must first be made clear that the death of Jesus was also of an eschatological nature, and that it agreed with the statements of the prophets concerning the final judgment connected with the Day of the Lord. It is in itself curious to note that in all three synoptic Gospels Jesus' discourse about the coming judgments which ring in the Day of the Lord, almost immediately precedes the story of the passion (Matt. 24; Mark 13; Luke 21). The Gospels give the impression that Jesus gave this discourse a few days before his death (Matt. 26.1f.). This is even more striking when we note that the same motifs repeat themselves in the great eschatological discourse and in the story of the passion. Jesus speaks of a flight and of a cooling of love; the passion story does the same. Jesus calls for vigilance; in Gethsemane this is repeated to the disciples, particularly Peter, James, and John. Jesus foresees a great oppression, and must later endure this himself. Jesus prepares for strange, natural phenomena such as an eclipse of the sun and an earthquake; and in the hour of death an eclipse takes place, while Matthew also mentioned an earthquake. In his conclusion Jesus foresees, after these terrible things, the appearance of the Son of Man on the clouds. After his death followed the resurrection and the appearances, and (according to Acts 1) his ascension on a cloud. These parallels cannot just be coincidental. They tell us that the Gospel writers, and primarily Jesus himself, believed that his death and resurrection ushered in the great Day of the Lord. This is also evident from Acts 2 where

Peter points to the description of the Day of the Lord in Joel 2. According to Joel, this will be ushered in by 'wonders in the heaven above and signs on the earth beneath' (Acts 2.19). Peter then introduced Jesus with a clear allusion to these words as 'a man attested to you by God with mighty works and wonders and signs' (Acts 2.22). The earliest generations of believers, immersed in the literature of the Old Testament, must have considered the prophecies about the last days fulfilled in the life, death, and resurrection of Jesus, in a manner now difficult for us to imagine. It might even be possible that they saw this in every detail of the gospel story. This now escapes us. It is, therefore, not impossible that the strange statement about the young man who, in the hour of trial, ran away naked (Mark 14.51f.) stands in direct connection with what Amos says about the coming judgment of Israel, 'And he who is stout of heart among the mighty shall flee away naked in that day, says the LORD' (2.16).[6] In any case, the donkey and Judas' thirty pieces of silver were viewed as fulfilment of Zechariah's prophecies concerning the last days.

What has been said about his death can also be said about his resurrection. It was the end of history, Yahweh's great victory over his enemies in which occurred what the apocalypse of Isaiah had foreseen—death was destroyed. Jesus repeatedly pointed to the fact that he should suffer and die, but also that he should be raised 'on the third day'. He borrowed this expression from the promise of Hosea, 'He has stricken, and he will bind us up. After two days he will revive us; on the third day he will raise us up, that we may live before him' (6.1f.). Jesus knew that he was the substitutionary remnant, in place of Israel and the world. The decrees concerning Israel and all nations centre in him as the only and actual partner in God's covenant with man. His resurrection is God's triumph over the adversaries, the act by which guilty man is raised and allowed to live before him. Thus, for Jesus, the resurrection must have been the beginning of the great Day of the Lord, following the Messianic woes of Golgotha. Jesus' confession before the

Sanhedrin here also speaks in clear tones. Now that the Messianic woes have reached their zenith in the rejection of the Suffering Servant, the Son of Man will soon appear in his divine glory. The prophecy of Daniel 7 is fulfilled in the resurrection. The conclusion of Luke seems to suggest that the resurrection and the ascension, as two closely connected phases of the great victory, took place on the same day.[7] Matthew does not do this, but ignores the ascension. He gives us, along with other words of the glorified Jesus, another reference to Daniel 7, 'All authority in heaven and on earth has been given to me' (28.18). This agrees with what is said about the Son of Man, 'And to him was given dominion and glory and kingdom' (Dan. 7.14).

History as God's struggle in Israel with the adversaries has come to an end—the Kingdom has come.

NOTES

[1] *The Kingdom of God and the Son of Man*, trs. Filson and Woolf, London, 1938.

[2] E. Stauffer, *New Testament Theology*, trs. J. Marsh, New York and London, 1956, p. 111.

[3] The rendering of the RSV footnote agrees more closely with the Dutch version used by the author; the RSV note is used in this paragraph for clarity. Cf. New English Bible. [*Trans.*]

[4] G. Schrenk in *TWNT* (I, pp. 608-12). I am in agreement with his conclusions.

[5] *Ibid.*, p. 612.

[6] Paul S. Minear, *Christian Hope and the Second Coming*, Philadelphia, 1953, ch. 10, 'A Naked Man'; p. 145: 'It is clear that Mark viewed Gethsemane as a day of judgment, with the young man doing what all men do on that day.' This is a stimulating book.

[7] See Luke 24.51. This is no doubt true if the addition of the 'Western Text' is original. It says: 'And he was taken up into heaven.'

4

JESUS CHRIST THE BEGINNING
OF HISTORY

He [Christ] is the culmination of the Old Testament, but also the
Firstborn of the new creature: not only ἀρχή and τέλος, alpha and
omega, but also, from another point of view, the τέλος-ἀρχή, the
end of one world and beginning of another, the turning-point of
history. This pattern is another of the distinguishing marks of the
Christian theology of history.

Jean Daniélou, *The Lord of History*, trans. Nigel Abercrombie,
Chicago, 1958, p. 195.

Naherwartung—*Dodd and Schweitzer*

IN THE preceding 'chapter we have seen that the Gospels are
full of *Naherwartung*.[1] With the intentional use of this (difficult to translate) German word we are reminded of the
important discoveries and controversies of New Testament
scholarship during the last half-century. We think particularly of Albert Schweitzer, and the Englishman C. H. Dodd.
Their names are symbols of opposite opinions; the first of
'consistent eschatology', and the other of 'realized eschatology'. Yet—the word 'eschatology', featuring in both views,
already points that way—they move on common ground
and their opinions have several points of agreement. Both
see the Gospels full of *Naherwartung*. The eschatological
Kingdom of God was brought nearer by Jesus, but the result
of this insight is different, even antithetical. For Dodd,
Jesus himself is the appearance of the long-awaited Kingdom.
Thus, for him, the Kingdom is a present reality among us
in and since Jesus—'realized eschatology'.[2] According to
Schweitzer the Kingdom was, in the expectation of Jesus, a

66

very near but strictly future entity. It is his opinion that Jesus did not bring the Kingdom, but expected and proclaimed it. His voluntary, sacrificial death was thus an attempt to bring the Kingdom nearer as a realization of the Messianic sufferings.[3] There are other variations connected with this fundamental difference. Dodd believes, for instance, that the images and expressions derived by Jesus from Jewish apocalyptic must be seen as just a convenient form for his witness concerning the present kingdom,[4] while Schweitzer views Jesus principally as an apocalyptist of the 'Enoch' type. We have already come to the conclusion that neither of the two opinions is correct. In one important aspect the two opposing positions lead to the same consequence—both are embarrassed by the fact that in Jesus' own words the synoptic Gospels already speak about a continuing history after his death and resurrection. Dodd finds proof in these words that the Kingdom was not meant to be an entity in history, but a 'timeless fact', an 'eternal order', in an almost Platonic sense of the word (almost, for this timelessness is the presentation of God's grace and judgment).[5] Schweitzer's school eliminates these words as not authentic; they are later additions of the Church to camouflage the fact that Jesus with his *Naherwartung* had become the victim of a mistake.[6] In this way, both opinions are in contradiction to the synoptic witness which, on this point, we explain as follows: Although the Kingdom of God had been brought near, and through the death and resurrection of Jesus had actually arrived, a new, earthly period followed which was not contradictory to but introduced by the Kingdom. Jesus is the end *and* the beginning of history; end *as well as* beginning. *Naherwartung*, indeed, but of the Kingdom in its mystery; of the Kingdom in the *Gestalt* of a historical period which stretches from the realization of the Kingdom, by means of Jesus' death and resurrection, to its still future unveiling.

Jesus' Prophecy Before the Sanhedrin

We again direct our attention to the words which sentenced Jesus to death: 'You will see the Son of man sitting at the right hand of Power, and coming with the clouds of heaven' (Mark 14.62). The challenging meaning of these words is made even plainer by Matthew and Luke, 'But I tell you, *hereafter* you will see the Son of man . . .' (Matt. 26.64). Jesus' death and resurrection ushered in the victory over the beasts and the taking over of power by the Son of Man. But this great event is not a once-for-all incident, or like a flash of lightning. It is extensive through time. Jesus' words are a combination of two quotations. As we have already noted, the second part draws from Dan. 7. The first half is an echo of Ps. 110.1: 'The Lord says to my lord: "Sit at my right hand, till I make your enemies your footstool."' The wording shows that the placing of the Lord (the king) at the right hand of God is not simultaneous with his definitive, public triumph, but that it precedes it. The early Church too had identified in that sense these words with Jesus, as is clear from the use of Ps. 110.1 in Acts and the Epistles. They saw these words fulfilled in the period between ascension and consummation.

Something else should be noted in the words of Jesus to the Sanhedrin. The text of Dan. 7.13 is not repeated exactly. There it states that the Son of Man came to God. 'He came to the Ancient of Days and was presented before him.' Jesus considered this coming, especially where it follows the quotation of Psalm 110, *not* as the coming of the Son of Man from the earth to God, but reversed: his return from God to the earth. This is not a contradiction. This return presupposes the coming which is already presumed in the quotation of Psalm 110. Even if an inversion, it is plain that in Daniel 7 (see verse 14) a return to the earth where all nations will serve him follows the coming of the Son of Man to God. Both Daniel and Jesus have a double movement in mind—from earth to God, and from God to earth. From the quotation of Psalm 110 it seems that Jesus places a span of time between the two movements; a period in which God has already given the power over nations to the Son of Man (see Matt. 28.18); but a time in which this has not yet been revealed by the return of the Son of Man to earth. The great Day of the Lord, then, consists of at least three acts: 1. the coming of the Son of Man to God; 2. his sitting at the right hand of God; and 3. his return in order to reveal his power over the world. The followers of the *Naherwartung* think exclusively about point 3, which they remove from its context in the New Testament.

'Hereafter you will see the Son of man seated at the right hand of Power, and coming on the clouds of heaven.' The Day of the Lord has arrived with the death and resurrection of Jesus. That Day will be revealed by visible signs, and will continue in an irreversible progress until the revelation of the Son of Man in glory. Fison makes the following observation on Jesus' words to the Sanhedrin,

> It is meant to be . . . a coming in the immediate future to be seen by anyone who had eyes to see it on Good Friday and on Easter day as well as on the day of Pentecost and right onward till the parousia. The future coming is only rightly understood as the final term of a whole series of comings.[7]

The Execution on Earth of Christ's Exaltation

An expression such as that the Son of Man will be seen from now on leads to the conclusion that his sitting at the right hand of God is not just a mysterious, heavenly reality, but that its working-out and effect must take place in earthly events and circumstances. There is no doubt about this in the New Testament. Great things take place on earth; things which are the visible aspects of the coronation of the Son of Man. When Jesus says (with Daniel 7 in mind) in Matt. 28.18 that 'all authority in heaven and on earth has been given to me', he follows it in verse 19 by saying, 'Go therefore and make disciples of all nations.' The connection made by the word 'therefore' is assumed to be considerably stronger than is usually the case. It must not be thought that since this power of the Son of Man had become a fact it must be proclaimed to all men. Rather, it meant above all that this power on earth becomes a fact through the proclamation of Christ to all nations. The missionary task itself is the earthly manifestation of Christ's glorification. It is clear from the parallel passage in Acts 1.6-8 that this word 'therefore' is to be taken in this stronger sense. There the disciples live in a typically Jewish apocalyptic *Naherwartung* which considered the end of the world at hand, the results of which will be that the people of the saints of the Most High (Dan. 7.27), namely Israel, will receive power over the world. Jesus tells them that it is not for them to know the seasons, and that its determining belongs to God alone, 'but you shall receive power when the Holy Spirit has come upon you; and you shall be my witnesses in Jerusalem and in all Judea and Samaria and to the end of the earth'. According to verse 3 this expression of Jesus concerns 'the things pertaining to the kingdom of God' [KJV]. Central to this are the outpouring of the Holy Spirit and its resulting missionary work.

The 'Little Apocalypse'

Yet the missionary endeavour, although the central sign, is not the only manifestation on earth of the arrival of the Day of the Lord. Even when we limit ourselves to the synoptic Gospels we will find many indications of the historical extent of the Day of the Lord; indications which make it clear that the Day is marked by many historical signs. Most striking in this connection is the so-called 'Little Apocalypse' found in Mark 13, Matthew 24, and Luke 21. This section presents several difficulties. The connection between its parts is often not clear. How much unity and connection is really there, and how much of it is a loose collection of utterances? Also, how many of these are Jesus' own words, and how many are additions and changes by the next generation? An answer based on exact study of the text cannot be given. The answers of the interpreters are repeatedly and strongly influenced by their total view of the eschatological content of Jesus' preaching. We approach these and other fragments with certain questions, but we are not primarily interested in the answers which have, or have not, been given. The Gospels repeatedly present to us the first generation's witness of their concept of history and the future on the authority of Jesus. We want to understand this witness. The Little Apocalypse is not an exception to, but an affirmation, ratification, and expansion of, the utterances which we can also find elsewhere. The introduction is like that found in Acts 1. In a tense *Naherwartung* the disciples asked about the last days (Mark 13.4). Jesus answered by preparing them for a new phase of history. Due to the many signs of the last days they were in danger of assuming that the end was in the near future. 'But the end is not yet' (vs. 7). This is only 'the beginning of the sufferings' (vs. 8). The missionary enterprise must first run its course (vs. 10). Only the Father knows when this season will end (vs. 32). For that reason two things are needed for the future— watchfulness (vss. 33-36) and perseverance (vs. 13). Here, too, the preaching of the gospel to all nations is an important sign of the new phase of history. Besides this, there are also signs of a negative nature—the many messiahs, the suffering of the persecuted Church, and throughout the world division between nations and natural disasters. When we ask for the cause of these negative signs, the Little Apocalypse points us to the future destruction of Jerusalem (vs. 2). Later on in the book we shall refute the popular notion that these predictions are not by Jesus, but additions of a later generation. In doing this we do not deny that the function of these predictions in connection with the Little Apocalypse does not present some difficult problems. But it is certain that the destruction of Jerusalem is one of the earthly signs of the fact that the Son of Man has taken over the power, and that it calls the other signs into action. This destruction in turn finds its cause in the fact that Jesus the Messiah was rejected by his own nation. This is strongly expressed in the parable of the vineyard (Mark 12.1-12), and in the parable of the great banquet (Luke 14.15-24). In addition to this, Israel must temporarily make room for the Gentiles; for the vineyard is given to others (Mark 12.9), and Jerusalem is trodden down 'until the times of the Gentiles are fulfilled' (Luke 21.24).

Expressions of Fernerwartung

It is no longer surprising that elsewhere in the Gospels we also find words which call to mind thoughts of *Fernerwartung*[8] rather than *Naherwartung*. It should also be noted that the Gospel writers place almost all these words in the last days before Jesus' arrest when it was already plain to him that Israel had rejected her Messiah. For that reason a short and speedy course to the Day of the Lord was now impossible. Now the servant would be in danger of thinking, 'My master is delayed' (Matt. 24.48). The maidens would fall asleep 'as the bridegroom was delayed' (Matt. 25.5). And they who would receive the talents must remember that the master returns 'after a long time' (Matt. 25.19). Luke states that Jesus told this parable 'because he was near to Jerusalem, and because they supposed that the kingdom of God was to appear immediately' (Luke 19.11).

Other words point less obviously in this direction. In Mark 2.19 Jesus prepares his disciples for the fact that the bridegroom will be taken away and that there will be a day of fasting, a day in which the Messianic hope will be hidden, a day of watching and suffering. In Mark 14.7-9 Jesus points to the future time when he will no longer be with his followers; a time in which the gospel is proclaimed and the poor will take the place of the Lord in the love of the Church. The parables in Matthew 13 about the weeds and the field, the mustard seed which becomes a tree, and the leaven which leavens all the meal, also point out that the Kingdom must go through a development (we do not shy away from the word), a development which will manifest itself partly in positive and partly in negative signs. Jerusalem is destroyed and the gospel goes into the entire world bypassing Israel because Israel has rejected her Messiah. It grows into a mighty force, but it also brings confusion and division. The Church is persecuted and will have to travel a hard road of suffering. All this does not mean a postponement of the Kingdom, but only a postponement of its consummation. It is the image in which the Kingdom appears in a sinful and broken world. It is the form in which the enthronement of the Son of Man at the right hand of Power in its first phase becomes visible on earth.

It is very possible that among these words are also elements of 'church theology' [*Gemeindetheologie*]. This is quite probable since the Gospels were written at a time when the words of Jesus were confirmed by experience. Conversely, these words were read in the light of experience. However, it is hardly probable that all of this originated only in the Church, and that it should be included in the Gospels in contradiction to Jesus' own words. We have no basis for this at all. We should then have to tamper in the most arbitrary manner with the words ascribed to Jesus. Whoever does this proves that he approaches these texts with a preconceived opinion of Jesus, and that he forcefully wants them to answer to this opinion. Every view of *Naherwartung* which does not make organic room for the elements of *Fernerwartung* judges itself by doing this. I hope to have shown that the elements of *Naherwartung* and *Fernerwartung* have an organic connection rather than being contradictory. The Kingdom is at hand, but in the *Gestalt* of the missionary enterprise and suffering it receives a duration in world history; the extent of this duration is unknown.

Three Problem Texts

With this conclusion we must not forget that there are a few expressions in the synoptic Gospels which seem to point in another direction, and from these it is suggested that Jesus saw the completion of the Kingdom at hand. If counted correctly, we are dealing with three texts (Matt. 10.23; Mark 9.1; and 13.30). These are few in comparison with the many texts in which we read about a clear tendency. We do not care whether these words are authentic and original, or whether the many texts which point in a different

73

direction are of a later time. Nor can we be satisfied with a far-fetched explanation, as is so often done in traditional exegesis. Since the disciples of consistent eschatology often call upon these words, much material has been written these last few years concerning these texts. We can make grateful and critical use of this.

First Matt. 10.23. This is a part of a discourse made when the disciples were sent out. They are promised division, hate, and persecution. Then verse 23: 'When they persecute you in one town, flee to the next; for truly, I say to you, you will not have gone through all the towns of Israel, before the Son of man comes.' Schweitzer explains that here Jesus sent his disciples on a short missionary journey, and that the fact that they returned without the Kingdom having arrived became the great crisis of his life. He became convinced through this that by his suffering and death he must call up the Messianic woes and suffer them, and in this way bring the Kingdom nearer. 'It should be noted that the non-fulfilment of Matt. 10.23 is the first postponement of the Parousia.'[9] This is not correct, however. Schweitzer confuses the sending in Matthew with that in Mark 6.7ff. The latter includes Israel only, and takes place in a very short time. No words are spoken in the spirit of Matt. 10.23. A little further it is simply recorded that the disciples returned after the completion of their assignment (Mark 6.30; Luke 9.1-6, 10). Matthew does not mention a return. This is not surprising because here the assignment has a much broader scope; the Gentiles are also included (vs. 18). Matthew included everything in this passage which is connected with the missionary task. Verse 23 falls here and has no parallel in the other Gospels. It is in close connection with the preceding words, 'he who endures to the end will be saved'. It contains an encouragement for the Jewish congregation (Matthew writes to them especially) which is being prepared for a terrible time of persecution. But that time will not be of long duration. There will be many opportunities to flee. The great deliverance will come before these possibilities are exhausted.

Mark 9.1 reads, 'And he said to them, "Truly, I say to you, there are some standing here who will not taste death before they see the kingdom of God come with power." ' The question is what Jesus had in mind. It is no longer possible for us to determine this with certainty. Some believe it points to the consummation. Others believe that the resurrection is meant. Still others believe that it points to all the events of the Kingdom which, from the cross and resurrection via Easter and the missionary endeavour, rush to the consummation. The matter is complicated even more by the fact that all three synoptics follow this expression immediately with the story of the transfiguration on the mountain. This proves that the Gospel writers—or at least the sources from which they worked—made a connection here; a connection which is more striking when we accept that it is not historical. It seems clear that the Gospel writers considered this expression fulfilled in Jesus' transfiguration on the mountain. 'Some' were allowed to be witnesses of this. The word 'some', however, could also have another nuance and mean that the eyewitnesses, as opposed to the world, could view and understand the signs of the arrival of the Day of the Lord (John 14.19; Acts 10.41).

Finally, Mark 13.30, 'Truly, I say to you, this generation will not pass away before all these things take place.' This expression, also, is not as simple as it would seem. What is the antecedent of 'all these things'? Probably the two preceding verses about the visible signs of the Kingdom, and not the consummation spoken of in verse 26. It would then be incomprehensible that two verses later it states that no one knows the day or the hour. Others introduce the possibility that the word translated as 'generation' should be understood as 'kind' or 'genre'. One could then think of 'this evil and perverse generation', but this makes no real sense. Or one could read 'this nation' (the nation of Israel) but such a promise of deliverance does not fit the context. One might, as some have done, sooner read an expression of the *Naherwartung* of the consummation. I believe, however, that here again we are dealing with the totality of the Kingdom which originates with Jesus, and leads to its fulfilment. This generation will still witness the dawn of the Kingdom in earthly reality.

When the three texts are taken together it is obvious how difficult it is to determine their meaning in the whole of the synoptic context. There are variations between the interpretations of all three, from the *Naherwartung* of Jesus' resurrection to the *Naherwartung* of the consummation. This 'vagueness' is entirely compatible with the fact that the New Testament views the Kingdom as history which spreads forcibly and develops rapidly. If the three texts look towards the consummation, it is clear that they still suggest a period of several decades preceding the consummation. There is no question of *Naherwartung* in the strict sense. It is possible that Jesus thought of the history of the Kingdom in terms of only a few decades. This cannot be said with certainty from these texts, but one can suspect it. Considering Jesus' other utterances about the long duration and about the fact that the end is unknown, it is unacceptable to believe that the idea of a fixed duration—e.g. a few decades—has had any real significance in his preaching. It was his conviction, however, that world history now leads directly to the consummation.

We can say no more without falling into fantasies. And it should be obvious that we include the popular notion that Jesus considered the consummation in the immediate future among the fantasies. This is even an understatement, for the notion is contradictory to the plain witness of the synoptics. Whoever persists in it creates a new problem; for how could the Christian congregation continue when it became evident that Jesus had made a mistake? This should at least have led to a great crisis. But not a trace is found of such a crisis in the New Testament, or in the writings of the next generation. One could mention II Peter 3.4 where men are introduced as saying, 'Where is the promise of his coming?' However, these are clearly set apart from the Church as 'scoffers'. The way the question was dealt with does not leave the impression that it played a central role in the life of the congregation.

The Naherwartung *of the Primitive Church*

It is not implied that the early Church was devoid of all *Naherwartung*. It was present in even clearer terms than in the case of Jesus himself. This is natural. When Jesus talked about the 'near' Kingdom, he thought about the event that lay still entirely before him and which would begin with his death and resurrection. But the primitive Church knew that she was already in that Kingdom. She had received the Spirit, had taken part in the missionary task, had been witness to the destruction of Jerusalem, had suffered, and had been persecuted. When she looked into the future, she looked to the consummation. She had a burning hope that it would come soon. One could say that there is room for a *Naherwartung* in the accepted, strict sense of the word only after Jesus' resurrection and ascension, and after the outpouring of the Holy Spirit. It appears to me that we can find traces of this in Paul. It is hardly possible to interpret Rom. 13.12; I Cor. 15.51f.; I Thess. 4.15-17 in any other way. This is, however, not surprising. It is more striking that in Paul we do not find a trace of crisis either when he later becomes used to the idea that he will fall asleep *before* the consummation. Whether the duration of the history of the Kingdom inaugurated by Jesus would be short or long, has never been an article of faith. They were seeing the Kingdom of God arrive in power. For that reason there was no place for any doubt in the consummation of this event. Even if they hoped that this take place soon, the fact that the period of waiting seemed longer did not lessen the assurance in which they walked in that Kingdom. The joy over the great Beginning removed all alarm over the delay of the End.

Jesus' Work as the Postponement of the End

When we remember what has been discussed in this chapter we must notice that Jesus, although rooted in the Old Testament, goes beyond the Old Testament and its view of the future. Through Jesus (not only in his opinions, but particularly through his death and resurrection) the *eschaton* becomes more extensive, and takes on the form of history. In this way Jesus was unique not only in comparison with the apocalyptists of his day who considered the final judgment as being at hand, but also in comparison with his nation and his own followers who did not count on the self-humiliation of the Suffering Servant, on a missionary task which was to be fulfilled in the world. When we ask for the cause of this difference, we must point to Jesus' love for sinners. The apocalyptists find it very normal that the judgment is near, and that only a small group of the elect of Israel will be saved. Jesus has compassion for the lost sheep of the house of Israel, and, still broader, for the Gentiles; the people on the highways and hedges outside the city of Israel (Luke 14.23). He did not desire a kingdom that would crush man. His coming as the Suffering Servant did not primarily mean the introduction of the judgment, as John the Baptist suggested (Matt. 3.10), but it meant the postponement of judgment, the creation of new history, a dispensation of grace and patience. And that not as a preparation for the Kingdom, but as a temporary form of that Kingdom. In this way the love of God already comes to dwell among a guilty humanity. Just a few people around Jesus understood this. Only he who understood that his own condemnation was the only thing he could expect from an imminent judgment, could understand the glory of this new proclamation of the Kingdom.

History as Analogy of the Christ-Event

This new history is not completely characterized by the words 'grace' and 'patience'. We have already seen that along with the positive signs of mission and growth, the negative signs of division and suffering are not lacking. It is clear that the positive signs stem from the fact of Jesus' triumph and exaltation, and these cause his love to become the great force in history. It is also clear that the division and suffering are connected with the division which took place over him, and with the suffering which became his lot. And the servant, indeed, is not greater than his Master. By this is meant that the event of the Kingdom brought into the world by Jesus is an analogue of what happened at that time in Palestine, when in Jesus the love of God came to dwell among guilty men. The suffering of the Church does not bring atonement. In their limitation and temporariness her victories are not of an eschatological nature in the sense of Jesus' exaltation. But of analogy we must speak. As the Head is, so also is the body. We can, then, also describe the event of the Kingdom which was set into motion by Jesus' cross and resurrection, and which is being realized throughout the world by the missionary endeavour, as *an analogy of the Christ-Event which is being realized throughout the world.* We believe that in these words we have expressed the core of the New Testament view of history. The rest of this book will be dedicated to the task of a broader explanation of this in the light of the many expressions on this point in the New Testament.

NOTES

[1] *Naherwartung*, a German word, is difficult to translate. Its approximate, but unsatisfactory, English translation is 'immediate expectation'. [*Trans.*]

[2] A good summary of Dodd's ideas may be found in his often reprinted book, which has been widely read: *The Parables of the Kingdom*, London, 1935.

[3] One finds the classical exposition of 'consistent eschatology' in Albert Schweitzer, *Geschichte der Leben-Jesu-Forschung*, Tübingen, 1913, ch. 21: 'Die Lösung der Konsequenten Eschatologie'—English version: *The Quest of the Historical Jesus*, New York, 1964. His most important follower is the historian of dogma from Bern, Martin Werner, who devotes the second chapter of the Introduction of the main work to these questions, *Die Entstehung des Christlichen Dogmas*, Bern-Leipzig, 1941, pp. 36-79.

[4] See Dodd, *The Authority of the Bible*, London, 1928. Although these forms 'preserve something essential to the idea' (p. 238), yet 'for us it is a scheme of thought, too fantastic to be taken seriously' (p. 202), and

moreover, 'it is almost certain that this element has been exaggerated by His reporters' (p. 236).

[5] See *The Parables of the Kingdom*, 1943, pp. 105-10.

[6] The position taken by Schweitzer and Werner has recently (from a different background) been defended and expanded by Bultmann and his followers, Hans Conzelmann, Erich Grässer, Willi Marxen, and Philip Vielhauer. It is their opinion that, like the apocalyptists, Jesus believed in an immediate end of the world; when this did not occur faith directed itself to that part of history which since the resurrection develops towards the consummation. In this development they give great importance to Luke who, especially in Acts, might have replaced, or at least supplemented, the vision of the 'end-history' by a 'salvation-history'. However, there are those who admit that there were already traces of this development in Mark and Matthew, and even in the oral traditions behind their Gospels. Oscar Cullmann contested these opinions in the *Theologisch Literaturzeitung* of January 1958, pp. 1-12, under the title, 'Parusieverzögerung und Urchristentum'. He, too, believes that the concept of salvation history was especially expanded by Luke. But he argues against the idea that it was created by him. It rests on concrete events, especially the resurrection, and behind these it rests on a tension between fulfilment *now* and consummation *later*, which Cullmann already finds present in Jesus in Matt. 11.4ff. 'The intensity of Jesus' *Naherwartung* confirms that the beginning is already a reality' (p. 10). Moreover, Cullmann considers the way in which Bultmann's school views many of the synoptic sayings as unauthentic to be arbitrary.

The problems with which the schools of Schweitzer and Bultmann struggle, originate from their fundamental dogma that in his eschatology Jesus was an apocalyptist. This dogma is denied by the New Testament, and has not been proven. For that reason we choose Cullmann's position as more real and less contrived. As we see in J. A. T. Robinson, *Jesus and His Coming* (London, 1957), the opposite view is held under the influence of Dodd; namely that Jesus concentrated on the present of his appearance, and that the apocalyptic sections in the Gospels are later additions of the Church. It is high time that all of these schools met in order, together, to set up norms by which some things can be proclaimed as 'scientific' and as 'conclusive'. Could the gentlemen not enter into what in physics is called 'complementary thinking'?

[7] J. E. Fison, *The Christian Hope: the Presence and the Parousia*, London, 1954, p. 193; see also pp. 190-94.

[8] *Fernerwartung*, another German word difficult to translate into English, is the opposite of *Naherwartung* and means approximately 'far expectation'. [*Trans.*]

[9] A. Schweitzer, *The Quest of the Historical Jesus*, New York, 1964, p. 360.

5

THE MISSIONARY ENDEAVOUR AS A HISTORY-MAKING FORCE

It should not be surprising that this dreadful virus, Christianity, has evoked certain reactions when it has been injected under the skin and even to the heart of pagan culture. Not only a novelty, but an enigma; at the same time consuming and insatiable. It is no longer a case of pleasant dreams of philosophers. It is a case of saying yes or no. No means the risk of eternal death. And yes means a certain transformation of the flesh and the soul which is terrifying to both.

Paul Claudel, *Pages de Prose*, Paris, 1949, p. 394.

THE WORLD has changed since the exaltation of Christ. It has become a part of the Kingdom, of history. This is a declaration of faith, but a declaration concerning the reality in which we now live. This reality, like all reality, can be explored in more than one way. The insight that it must be explained in light of the exaltation of Christ and the dawning of the Kingdom cannot be forced on anyone but remains a declaration of faith. However, gazing on Christ, we believe that only through him can we know the decisive guidelines in our history. Is this a kind of Christian philosophy of history? We are not afraid of that word. And if we still avoid it, it is because we wish to keep ourselves as close to theology as possible. At the close of this chapter we wish to retranslate what we first stated in cultural-philosophical terms into the terms of the message of the New Testament, and express it in such a way that much of what at first glance could be considered a more or less independent philosophy of history forms an organic part of the apostles' proclamation of Christ.

81

Christ the Meaning of History

The Times Without History

At the beginning of this book we noted that outside of
Israel and the New Testament there has been little or no
awareness of a concept of history. It should be clear that no
reproach was meant in this observation. The understanding
of history was lacking because the facts were lacking. Only
when Yahweh appeared on the horizon was man radically
set free from nature, placed on a road, and led to a goal.
Outside this event, man is bound to nature. He lives by its
cycle and in general by that which is, by the dicta of nature,
and from the experience of a social ordering given by nature.
Tribal society—or the family, the caste, the state—determines his life. And these again direct themselves to the sun
and the rain, to the position of the stars, to life and death,
to the seasons and the laws which govern the fertility of the
earth. Man, the community as well as the individual, knows
that he is caught in this great association. He has his small
but important place in it. Led by the forces which he honours
as gods, he can also influence these to some extent by sacrifices and magical actions. But his sphere of influence is very
limited. There is very little room for action in the circle of
fate. He who knows his limitation and lives by the laws of
the divine 'All' has a determined and harmonious life. The
large naturalistic cultures and even more the primitive
tribal cultures, rightly give us the impression of great
harmony, at any rate infinitely greater than that which we
now know.[1]

Greece and Rome, spiritually led by Greece, are different.
This is true, at least, on the surface. Both cultures are steeped
much deeper in ancient naturalism than was supposed, for
instance, by the Renaissance and Classicism. But all cultures
are characterized and guided by a thin upper stratum. This
stratum has, since about 1000 BC, freed itself from the
power of nature. Man himself became the measure of things.
Action—thinking must be included—wins great victories at
the expense of fate. This enormous change at origin within
the history of man's 'becoming' can no longer be undone,

and its influence can be felt to this day. Our modern world is unthinkable without Greece. One might even ask whether the influence of the proclamation of Christ in the world is thinkable without the background of the Graeco-Roman emancipation. And yet this emancipation did not lead to a change in the foundation of the structure of life. These cultures never withdrew from existence under the natural forces.

For the Greek Logos seeks its foundation and its justification (that is its greatness and depth) in the forces which hold the mythical world in its eternal order, and which also surround with superior forces the mighty human spirit itself.[2]

Yet there have been conflicts of which the conflict around Socrates is the best-known example. But even the most emancipated thinkers repeatedly accommodated themselves, if not to the thinking of the people, at least to the structure of life based upon it. They could do no other, since man's emancipation in regard to nature presents in itself no alternative possibility on which life can be built. This depends on the power to which finite man is oriented, and on which he relies in order to free himself from the forces of nature. Greek and Roman cultures did not find such a new and common superhuman point of reference. In the end, life was again determined by the laws of the Greek polis or Roman state. It is true that these to a greater extent than in the older cultures were considered as an object of man's activity, but they were still fundamentally experienced as forces of nature. At any rate, the Greek Enlightenment did not penetrate this, although naturalism did not hinder the Enlightenment.

However, we must beware lest we judge this naturalistic way of life only negatively. Wherever the God who is above all forces and who controls all forces is not known, the predetermination of man in the events of nature is the guarantee that life will not end in chaos. Man's emancipation from nature is fatal if it is an end in itself. It will eventually lead man into a vacuum, and disintegrate life. In the Bible naturalistic paganism is positively appreciated in more than one place. This is most obvious in Gal. 4.1-3 where man is included among the 'powers' as a minor who must remain under guardianship and supervision as long as Christ does not raise him to adulthood. Weaker, but just as positive, is Rom. 3.25 which describes the pre-Christian era as 'in his divine forbearance', and Acts 17.26f., which states that God has for all nations 'determined allotted periods and the boundaries of their habitation, that they should seek God, in the hope that they might feel after him and find him'.

The Missionary Endeavour Leads to Freedom

We stated that before the appearance of Christ the world outside of Israel had no history. What we meant by that can also be expressed by saying that at that time the world did not know freedom. We must, however, make a differentiation, as with the concept of history. In a certain general sense, man even then possessed freedom. In opposition to the animal, man is on his way; he is transcendent (existential), he follows after ideals, he overcomes adversity, he creates culture. This is true of man in all times. In a general sense, man has always been aware of history as a result of his self-realization.

But in the Bible, the word 'freedom' has a very special meaning. It signifies the possibility and call of man to direct himself to God and to choose him; and then in this way as a child of God, also to be brother to other men, and lord of nature. This is the highest and real freedom which is the foundation of, and integrates, all other forms of freedom. It is a possibility only when God makes himself known and draws man into his light. But there comes also, on the part of man, the dark shadow of the possibility to use this freedom against God, to emancipate himself from God, and to be as God himself. In reality this means to make freedom a slave in the service of the 'I' and the world. We see this magnificent and terrifying possibility and reality of freedom in Genesis 2 and 3.

This possibility and reality were unknown in the world of paganism. Freedom existed, of course, in the sense of cultural self-realization and in the daily choices from several possibilities. But this took place within an existence which itself was subject to a tribal or state community, to the powers of ancestors and family, to the social structures received from the past, and to the laws of the stars and seasons. The existing order was considered as the will of the gods and, as such, sacred. Whoever chose against this sacred reality (but who could continue in this long? What *else* could he choose?) pronounced his own death sentence, as soon as the choice was more than a private preference. It was different with the Greeks. Freedom was very broad, man was discovered as the adversary of the powers; but it does not lead beyond a vacillation between man and the powers of nature, in which the latter should eventually win. We are thinking of the growing religiosity and the emperor worship during the 'twilight of paganism'.

Man's awakening to freedom mentioned in Genesis 2 cannot take place as long as he 'is under guardians and trustees' (Gal. 4.2), but only (for that is the plain contrast to guardianship) when the proclamation concerning Jesus Christ reaches him. In him, a new God is introduced to the world, a God who is not identical with nature, nor with what is, nor with man, but the God who has created all things, and keeps it by his word, and who at the same time limits it, depriving it of its quasi-absoluteness. His appearance means the desacralization of existence. But this desacralization does not take place automatically. It occurs in and through the proclamation. The proclamation is not dictatorial; nor does it communicate truths which exist outside of it. Truth occurs through it, and truth approaches the listeners, enlisting and winning them. Proclamation neither constrains nor leaves man uninvolved. It makes a call, it invites us to arise and walk a new way. This is how it respects our freedom. No, this is putting it too mildly. The Lord who comes to us in the proclamation in this way calls our freedom to life. The freedom of choice finally finds its primary purpose, and all other choices can group themselves around this. Only now is the situation of Genesis 2 being realized for all nations. The tree of the knowledge of good and evil is planted in the paradise of immaturity. A new change at origin in the process of man's 'becoming' is introduced which is infinitely more radical and fruitful than that brought by Greece. Man now stands before the decision whether to remain bound to the powers of nature as a slave, or whether to join the Lord whose power and love delivers us from the earthly shackles, and who gives us a new life as children of God, and as lords of the world. We are here reminded of the conclusion of Matthew's Gospel, 'All authority in heaven and on earth has been given to me. Go therefore and make disciples of all nations' (28.18, 19a). This 'make disciples' (the parallel in Mark 16.15 says 'preach') is the work of the missionary proclamation. It is the primary and fundamental *Gestalt* of the Kingdom: *the* sign that power has been taken over by Christ. In an entirely new sense, man is called to choice and decision—to freedom.

This revolutionary power of the missionary proclamation is splendidly illustrated in the story of Paul's preaching in Athens, found in Acts 17. This city was the symbol of the highest point attainable to man without Christ. Yet, man was not able to effect complete equilibrium between himself and the powers of nature. There remained incalculable factors. That is the reason for the altar to the unknown God. And the city had not come to real history. The intellectuals of Athens are vividly described as spending 'their time in nothing except telling or hearing something new' (vs. 21). As long as the 'New' had not arrived they reached from the ancient and repetitious events for anything new, and because this too was soon old there was no end to the reaching and searching. Paul calls this existence 'the times of ignorance' (vs. 30), and proclaims that God now puts an end to these times 'because he has fixed a day' (vs. 31). On that day, the world will be ruled by one whose authority for this is derived from his resurrection from the dead (vs. 31). In view of that resurrection behind them, and that day before them, the Athenians are now called to decision and conversion (vs. 30). The account then ends with the statement that the listeners after hearing this unheard-of message fell into three categories: those who responded affirmatively, those who said No, and those who refused to make a decision, or at least postponed it (vs. 32). A small group accepted the faith (vs. 34). In spite of the small number, by this fact Athens was called to freedom, and in this way included in history.

The New Order of Life

With the words 'proclamation', 'freedom', and 'history' everything essential has been said about the change at origin which arises with the coming of the Kingdom. But these words signify but the centre of a gigantic circle. Or, stated more biblically, the Kingdom is like a mustard seed which grows into a tree, like leaven which leavens all the meal. It penetrates into the darkest corners of life, and creates a new order of life, together with a new appreciation for life. This takes place first in the Church of Christ. The so-called 'domestic rules' in the apostolic letters bear witness to this (Eph. 5 and 6; Col. 3; I Peter 2 and 3). As soon as the Church begins to exert its influence outside herself as a creative minority, the Kingdom also begins to uproot the life of an entire nation or a whole culture. Of course, this does not happen all at once, and it does not proceed everywhere at the same speed or to the same extent. In the ancient world before Constantine, when the Christian Church was persecuted, it happened hardly at all. After Constantine it moved faster, but even then the centuries-old pagan society was influenced deeply only in a few points (especially by philanthropic work). In Europe, the new order of life moved much more rapidly after 600. And in the nineteenth and twentieth centuries in the mission fields it moved at an almost breathtaking speed. But these historical differences stand removed from the main point. Wherever the Kingdom is introduced it uproots the world deeply, creates a new

order of life and a new appreciation for life. We now want
to describe this order in some detail.

The Lord who makes his entrance into the world through
the missionary proclamation is the Redeemer who comes to
seek and save what is lost. He comes not to be served, but to
serve. He seeks the single sheep, he has compassion for the
poor, he heals the sick, and he forgives sinners. And the man
who through the proclamation is called to freedom begins
to reflect some of these divine attributes in his humility,
consciousness of guilt, self-denial, and readiness to forgive
and serve. Thus, a new idea of *being human* is ushered in; it
is not the proud humanity of the Greeks, but the humanity
of humility. The individual is recognized in his own significance. The human *personality* is respected. Particular attention is given to the suffering and oppressed. An ordinary
street scene, such as an ambulance stopping all traffic
because *one* wounded man must be transported, is the result
of the coming of the Kingdom. With these revolutionary
ideas is connected the concept of *being responsible*; that is, to
be answerable (to Someone), to render an account, and in
connection with this the idea of *coming of age*. *Inwardness* is
also a reality the ancient world did not know, because there
man lives in his relation to the natural forces. Only the
relationship of the individual to the one personal God
creates a personal, inward-reaching relationship. Augustine,
in his *Confessions*, was the first great interpreter of this, and
without it modern European literature and psychology, for
instance, and that typically European phenomenon, the
autobiography, would be unthinkable.

All this is against the natural 'life concepts' of man
dominated by the powers of nature. Ideas such as responsibility, humility, consciousness of guilt, service, etc., create
a gulf between what man ought to be and what he is. A
deep *awareness of norms* is developed, coupled with a *dissatisfaction* with the existing world, which can no longer be
appreciated as the expression of the divine will. They begin
to resist whatever does not conform to the norms. The
battle is pitted against exploitation, injustice, and slavery,

and against everything which is not motivated by love. The idea of social justice so well-known to us was injected by the missionary proclamation. We believe that although this justice does not eliminate the differences among men, it does lessen them. The Bible has taught us this also (Year of Jubilees, manna, II Cor. 8.1-15). Without these notions, our democracy (which is infinitely more democratic than that of Athens) and our social institutions are unthinkable.

But what actually is thinkable without the proclamation of Christ? Even *marriage* has undergone a fundamental change because of it. Monogamy, as a reflection of the love of Christ and the Church, has become the only possibility (Eph. 5). It presupposes that the wife is no longer seen as object, but as subject in a relationship of mutual maturity. Thus, marriage is no longer only an institution, but it is at the same time a very personal encounter. *Sexuality*, for the naturalistic concept of life no more than the ability to take part in the divine creation of life, now becomes mundane and is primarily appreciated as the expression of personal love between man and wife.

The new Lord brings *history* into the world. Since him, we see ourselves on a road to a goal. That which is does not coincide with that which is meant to be. Life has received the *Gestalt* of a goal-directed aspiration. In that life the powers of nature are desacralized, particularly the power which had been considered most sacred—that of the *state*. 'The most important and remarkable thing produced by history since Christ is the revelation of the real significance of the state' (Gunning). The statement, 'We must obey God rather than men' (Acts 5.29) has dethroned the state. *Tolerance*, too, is a (late) product of the Christian proclamation. It is rooted in the patience of God and in the character of the proclamation.

Nature must be mentioned immediately after the state. More than anything else, it was for ancient man the *Gestalt* of divine fate under which he had to place himself. Whoever violated nature called the wrath of the gods against him. Tilling the soil was almost all man was permitted to do, and even that had to be surrounded by rites and sacrifices. This went on until the Bible arrived and declared that God is not on the side of nature against man, but on the side of man against nature (Gen. 1.26-28; Ps. 8). Nature was desacralized and made the object of man's exploitation. In the missionary proclamation modern natural science and technology were in principle given. Qualitatively and quantitatively these differ greatly from what can be considered as their analogues in the ancient world. Technology is a result of the Kingdom. Through this, and in connection with the notion of history, develops a new ethos of *labour*. This was despised in the ancient world. We still find this view of life in many Eastern nations. This is unavoidable when deity is considered to be static like an 'Unmoved Mover' (Aristotle). Since Yahweh who 'is working still' (John 5.17) entered our lives through his actions, and included us in his history, work has taken on new meaning, and not to work is a vice. We could continue in this vein, but only one thing more must be mentioned. The concept of the *world as a unity*, too, we have not so much received from Greece (where it existed among small groups of Stoics), but from Israel and through the missionary proclamation. This occurs in the encounter with the Creator of the whole world, who, disregarding all boundaries, gathers the new people of God. The missionary endeavour is the first fundamental worldwide work. The significance for the world of European culture can be understood only against this background. The existence of the United Nations is rooted in this Christian concept.

All this has become so obvious to us that we no longer remember how we came by it, and often make the mistake of thinking that these ideas are natural, i.e. that they are a part of being human. It is a fact that much of the above was in greater or lesser degree already anticipated by the Greeks, and existed with the Stoics. The Stoics, however, remained only a small intellectual 'upper crust'. Early Christian writers rightly pointed out that it was the Christian Church which translated these ideas into forceful, cultural factors. In order fully to understand the unprecedented revolution that being human experienced through the proclamation of Christ, one must have lived in a communistic world, in the lands of Islam, in Hinduism, or among primitive people.

Secularization as a Christian and Antichristian Phenomenon

The inescapable and freedom-giving result of the missionary proclamation brings with it the two-sided phenomenon of the emancipation of man and the desacralization of natural existence. The new Lord who is declared to man as the saviour of sinners and victor over the forces of nature, by man's obedience to him, delivers man from obedience to nature and from the social institutions derived from the forces of nature. Christ brings the humanization of man and the materialization of nature. If we keep in mind the cultural and historical meaning of the concept of secularization, we might say, without being guilty of a play on words, that Christ secularized life.

Secularization is conversion projected in culture—the Christianization of life. Compared with the old existence it means an unknown freedom which can no longer be undone, even if only due to the fact that no one now can desire that. Secularization as the result of a conversion to Christ is sooner or later, to a greater or lesser extent, accepted by everyone regardless of whether he himself experiences this conversion to Christ, or whether he considers himself a part of the Christian Church. The acceptance of this Christianization or secularization is general, and a matter of course. This is not true of faith in Christ. Wherever the missionary endeavour has gone, the curious situation arises that a whole nation gratefully eats of the fruit, but only a minority desires the tree which produces the fruit. Many try to forget or deny from which tree these fruits are derived. They make the fruit an end in itself. They are concerned with the humanization of life as an end in itself. Now that the missionary proclamation has broken the power of naturalism and cleared the field of culture, they want consistently and above all else to continue what was begun in Greece. This is possible only through a faith in the *autonomy of man* which was begun in Greece, and which sooner or later is called into existence by the missionary proclamation. For wherever the missionary message penetrates, not only does Genesis 2 come to life, but Genesis 3 also. Whenever freedom is awakened in this fallen world, there will also be a misuse of freedom. Man listens to the voice which tells him that he might just as well, or better, use this God-given freedom against God, that he can be like God, and that he himself can determine what is good and what evil. Thus, secularization as a deliverance of life can move in two directions. The prisoner of nature can become a child of God in his maturity, or he can just as well take the role of a false god. Even this second possibility is due to the missionary proclamation. The proclamation involves risks which did not exist until now, and which are of grave proportions. Secularization is the child of the gospel, but a child who sooner or later rises against his mother. And yet, the mother would not be what she ought to be if she did not desire the child. The fact remains that the missionary endeavour calls into existence the greatest forces and counterforces. The autonomy of man takes place simultaneously with the enthronement of Christ.

This antichristian twist of secularization can be illustrated by all the phenomena characteristic of the Christianization of life. The awareness of norms becomes an autonomous, often utilitarian, ethic, which spells its own downfall. Social justice degenerates into a forceful assertion of real or supposed interests of groups and classes. Through the missionary proclamation sexuality—which in naturalism was a divine force, belonged to a sacred sphere, and was at once holy and natural—has become a normal earthly phenomenon, whose stimulation is being exploited, and whose meaning is being betrayed by exhibitionism. Marriage, which has become a very personal encounter, tends to lose its institutional character, and be viewed only as an expression of sometimes passing erotic emotions.

In the first chapter we noted that the concept of the meaning of history develops into a feverish striving for self-realization which ends up in a coarse evolutionism. The state with its sacred halo tends to lose its authority and become a toy of the factions who, in the name of democracy, lead to anarchy. Tolerance becomes colourless and purposeless, or leads to tyranny by the majority. Technology, meant to make nature the servant of man, becomes itself the enslaving power of man. The greatest mark of our autonomy also becomes its greatest threat. And labour, which has become honourable, threatens to grow into a false god who drives us on endlessly, now that he has been separated from the labouring God who gives man, his co-worker, a share in his sabbatical rest. Thus, secularized life becomes the great enemy of the theocratic order of life, as much as, or even more than, the naturalistic pattern of life had been.

Yet, secularism cannot deny its theocratic origin. If it did this, it would be 'cutting off the branch on which it is sitting'. For in itself it has no power to exist. This it receives from the tree of which it is the fruit. For that reason precisely the most antichristian representatives of secularized life are—unconsciously and even consciously—positively or negatively—dependent on the Christian faith. Wherever the missionary endeavour has made an impression on the culture, no active thinking or deeds are conceivable which are not positively or negatively dependent on the life-giving forces brought into the world by Christ. The rejection of the Christian faith, too, keeps its character of negation and, as such, remains completely in the circle of theocracy. Nietzsche is the classic example of this. But modern secular literature is full of these phenomena. Even atheism is no exception to this. European atheism is a typical 'Christian' phenomenon. 'Deity is rejected on the bases of the norms he himself introduced' (Miskotte)—namely, the norms of love and justice, to which the world does not apparently measure up. What is true in a negative sense is true also in a positive sense. The conviction that culture has a Christian source becomes evident to leading figures particularly during cultural crises. There is a suspicion that removal from the source should lead to desiccation and emaciation, to anarchy and nihilism. For that reason, for instance, modern novels and poetry seem surprisingly full of indications of the reign of Christ. In an author's entire work these indications are often inconsequential or erratic passages, and, for that reason, are more striking.

It should already be evident from all this, that the relationship between theocracy and secularization is very complicated. One moment they are identical, the next they are each other's sworn enemy. And even in the latter case they belong together, and are inseparably connected with each other. The Christian Church seldom does justice to this peculiar relationship. According to a cheap Roman Catholic notion the Reformation was the forerunner of antichristian secularization. In saying this, they forget not only the Reformation's hard struggle with secularization since Luther's break with Erasmus, but also the fact that this secularization was begun, not with the Reformation, but much earlier—the fourteenth century at the latest (nationalism and early Renaissance). The Protestant notion which makes the French Revolution the scapegoat of secularism is not worth much more. For the most noble cause of the French Revolution was that taken up against the Jesuits and absolute monarchy; and these are admittedly positive consequences of the missionary proclamation. It is impossible to divide Christian and antichristian secularization by a date. Christian secularization has until now not come to a standstill, and continues to win new territories. We need only to mention the abolition of slavery in the last century, and the struggle for the human rights of citizens (French Revolution), worker, woman, and coloured races. The eighteenth-century Enlightenment, too, with its battle against various forms of immaturity, superstition, and intolerance, has a pronounced positive Christian side. Inversely, there were already during the Middle Ages, particularly during the Renaissance, many evidences of antichristian secularization. The latter gained a grip on European culture since the fourteenth century, while in less mature centuries it was suppressed. Both Christian and antichristian secularization were, in principle, continually at work, and in practice were often hardly distinguishable.

We must now pause for a moment to note the peculiar fact that also in laudable secularization, at least during the last three centuries, it was not the believer, but the non-Christian who stood in the forefront. The Christian Church limited the secularization of life primarily to marriage and the family, respect for labour, expansion of basic knowledge, and charitable work on behalf of unfortunate groups. The change in the sacred character of the state has been unsatisfactory, the practice of tolerance has been negligible, natural science and technical development have been viewed with suspicion, superstition has been contained rather than attacked (witch-hunts), etc. One must not blame this on banal backwardness. The Church knew that Genesis 3 followed Genesis 2. Intuition suggested that an extension of secularization would inevitably lead to the disintegration of culture. That is why the Church repeatedly tended to be the protector of the old naturalistic ways of life. This defence of the existing order as the holy will of God was the outcome of man's century-long attempt to connect the proclamation concerning Yahweh with the ancient pagan concepts about deity as a static force, and the personification of fate. The Church herself never quite outgrew naturalism. That is why the mother has always been afraid of the child she bore. The Church walks on a narrow road: on the right threatens the slavery of the forces of nature, and on the left the anarchy of autonomous life. The Church has always been more afraid of the left than the right. We must not be too harsh in our criticism. The risks of secularization have, indeed, always been greater than those of naturalism whose shackles have been broken since the missionary proclamation.

Too often, however, the child was thrown out with the bath water, so that others who had their existence not in Christ but in human autonomy, were called to draw the missionary proclamation to its legitimate consequences. We say 'were called' because here, too, the Holy Spirit was at work. He performs his work through the Church, but also through what we call the world. The Church has created a type of man who learns to turn to God as a child to the Father, but for the rest he stays greatly involved in the institutions, traditions, and natural laws. And the Renaissance, humanism, the Enlightenment, and the nineteenth century have created a type of man who emancipated himself from all this, and became the lord of nature; but all too often the relationship to God as a child to the Father can no longer be found. In both we find the work of God's Spirit and the work of evil.

And if then we choose in favour of the Church because she has held fast to the 'one thing' which 'is needful' (Luke 10.41) and which was neglected by the world, we must remember clearly not only that the world is taught about God through the Church, but also that the Church is taught about God through the world. At this point there is a striking difference between Roman Catholicism and the Reformation. The first is inclined in theory and in practice to the naturalistic patterns of life (emphasis on institution and authority, immaturity, desire to return to the Middle Ages, difficulty with tolerance, room for superstition and popular belief, etc.). The second greatly extended Christian secularism, with the result that it had less resistance against antichristian secularism. But it also went deeper into the related questions; Roman Catholicism often profited from this. The typical Roman Catholic country is still either not sufficiently delivered from naturalism (Southern Europe and South America), or in strong reaction to this, has fallen into antichristian secularization (France, the South-European and South American intelligentsia). Protestant countries are much more secularized, but the Christian content of secularization has remained much higher (Scandinavia, Germany, Britain, the Netherlands, and the United States).[3]

The struggle between Christian and antichristian secularization has never been decided. It cannot be decided in this dispensation. Both remain intertwined, because the Church does not wish to return to naturalism, and the secularized world does not wish to move ahead to anarchy and nihilism. Sometimes the latter seems unavoidable. When this occurs, movements arise with a view to restore the old powers. But then it becomes evident that after Christ there is no return to these powers. They lead to a slavery which we now can no longer bear. Thus, whenever the threat of a restoration of life under the tyrannical powers arises, Church and world stand united for the same cultural values. But when the threat is past they seem to be each other's sworn enemy as two opposite poles of the theocratic pattern of life. Wherever the gospel has gone, a free, but intrinsically conflicting culture has arisen. The inner schism of our European and American culture is often noticed. But it is usually explained by the fact that we exist from two or more heterogeneous qualities, namely the missionary proclamation and the culture of Greece and Rome (perhaps also German tradition). It occurs to me that this is an unsatisfactory explanation. It is a matter of more cultures which give evidence of a union of heterogeneous traditions. Greece itself with its tension between an undertone of naturalism and an overtone of enlightenment, is one of these. The inner conflict would also have arisen without the influence of ancient culture. It is inherent in the missionary proclamation. On the one hand, the proclamation introduces the powers of the gospel into the world of nations. On the other hand, it sets free the demonic power of self-deification. In this way, it hurls the world into a schism which, before Christ, was unknown during the tyrannical harmony of paganism.

Thus far we have limited ourselves to European-North American culture. For was it not here that the consequences of the missionary proclamation were made explicit to a larger degree than anywhere else? It is difficult to discuss other developments which are still in the preliminary stages. But we cannot close this section without mentioning the strange happenings taking place among the Asiatic nations, and which are now beginning also in Africa. Imposing naturalistic patterns of life have often reigned for centuries. Usually the missionary activity existed there not much longer than a century, although it often deeply influenced the higher culture through its educational institutions (Japan, India, and elsewhere). Europe and America now flood these areas with all the products of a Christian and antichristian secularization. And these are grafted on what are still primarily naturalistic, tribal forms. But the tree, on which these fruits organically belong, is hardly transplanted at all. This means that the people who come in contact with the results of our culture are uprooted by it. The positive background—confrontation with the new Lord—is lacking. The help offered by the West presupposes an appreciation for labour, history, and nature, for which there is hardly room, for instance, in the acosmic philosophies of Hinduism and Buddhism.

Secularization is here divorced from its theocratic background, and hangs in the air. In this way it can actually lead to nothing but anarchy and nihilism. The highly praised aid to underdeveloped areas seemingly becomes a material blessing, but in reality it is a spiritual assault. Many of those who do this work seem to have little realization of this problem. They evidently do not know the meaning of the naturalistic way of life, nor are they acquainted with the counterforces which must deliver man from this. They are surprised when they see the lack of gratitude and success. And they do not at all understand the great confusion they create in the hearts of men, because they are no longer aware of the Christian presuppositions of their own culture. Where will all this end? It will end either in a destructive nihilism, or in a conscious quest for Christ who came to secularize life, and in whose service only, this secularized life is protected from nihilism. But if the latter is to be realized as the only beneficial possibility, then— along with the aid to underdeveloped areas—the proclamation of Christ must be resumed with unmatched force (by the young Churches, missions, and the world Church). Without this antidote, the present-day inoculation can only present us with serious diseases.

The Missionary Endeavour as a History-Making Force

The Double Mystery

In conclusion we return to the introductory words of this chapter. What has been presented here in terms of a Christian philosophy of culture is a part of the primitive Christian proclamation, and can be retranslated into its terms. We do this with the help of II Thessalonians 2. Paul writes to the congregation at Thessalonica which was seemingly disturbed by speculations concerning an imminent completion of history. The apostle reminds them that the antichrist must first come. Then he continues in verse 5, 'Do you not remember that when I was still with you I told you this?' This is noteworthy. To Paul the instruction concerning the coming antichrist seemed to have belonged among the fundamental truths of the faith which were to be impressed upon a young congregation. And according to the words, 'and you know what is restraining him now' (we will discuss this in another connection), this missionary instruction implied still more— a complete Christian view of history. We are now far removed from this. Paul then presents the antichrist in a broader sense when he says in verse 7, 'For the mystery of lawlessness is already at work.' He means that this has been the case since Christ's coming and the outpouring of the Holy Spirit. The word 'mystery' (*musterion*) usually signifies the salvation brought by Christ (e.g. Mark 4.11; Col. 2.2; I Tim. 3.16). In Pauline writing 'mystery' in that sense is almost the accepted expression. Now the same word signifies the power of the antichrist, who seemingly has come into operation together with the great mystery of Christ. The antichrist of the future will be the ripe fruit of the movement which is already in progress. For, 'as you have heard that antichrist is coming, so now many antichrists have come; therefore we know that it is the last hour' (I John 2.18). Christ and the antichristian power form together the *Gestalt* taken by the Kingdom in this guilty and broken earthly existence. The nature of the antichristian power is human self-deification (II Thess. 2.4) and blindness where the truth of God is concerned (vs. 11). This power is still a

99

musterion; that is, a hidden activity, behind masks, and often insolubly connected with the powers of Christ.

For Paul this was seemingly not an optional, private view of history, but an essential element of his proclamation. He had not learned this through an analysis of historical reality, but he had found it through the appearance of the Lord himself who had been set for the fall and rising of many and for a sign that is spoken against (Luke 2.34), who sows the good seeds, and who made the evil One sow the wrong seed (Matt. 13.24ff.), the Lord who was crucified and resurrected in this world. Paul is aware of the double mystery because he is aware of the twofold influence of Christ on this world. The certainty wherewith he speaks about the mystery of history in II Thessalonians 2 and elsewhere rests on this fact.

Here we come to the same conclusion as that of the preceding chapter: The result of the missionary proclamation is the realization throughout the whole earth of the analogy to the cross and resurrection of the Christ-Event. In this chapter we have attempted to translate this into terms of modern theory of culture. We are taught this not by the cultural-historical experience itself, but by the crucified and risen Lord. In the light of his appearance history becomes transparent for us to its ultimate depths. This two-sided character of history will be expanded in the chapters which follow.

NOTES

1 In this connection and for this whole chapter see my book, *Christus en de Machten*, Nijkerk, 1953 (English: *Christ and the Powers*, Scottdale, 1962), where these matters are developed by the exegesis of the concept of 'powers' in Paul.

2 F. Gogarten, *Verhängnis und Hoffnung der Neuzeit: Die Säkularisierung als theologisches Problem*, Stuttgart, 1953, p. 95.

3 Since I wrote this book much has changed on the Roman Catholic side!

6

THE CRUCIFIED CHRIST IN HISTORY

Jesus will be in agony until the end of the world; it is necessary
not to sleep during this time.

Blaise Pascal, *Pensées*, Brunschvicg ed., No. 553.

THE CONCLUSIONS of the preceding chapter might leave
the impression that they were too quickly drawn. It is true
that wherever Christ is introduced through the missionary
endeavour a split comes into life, and life receives the mark
of division and struggle. But does this necessarily mean that
life also receives the mark of Christ's suffering? Must Christ
succumb in this struggle? One could also view the result of
his coming differently. He could, for instance, be considered
the victor who, although he calls the counterforces to life,
also keeps them under control; or he keeps them under so
that there is an undecided (perhaps even undecidable)
balance of power of the opposing forces.

Suffering as the Reverse Side of the Fellowship with Christ

There is no doubt that the New Testament places in the
foreground the certainty that Christ, who brings not peace
but the sword (Matt. 10.34), repeatedly suffers defeat at the
hands of the counterforces he himself called to life. This
'sombre' image is doubtlessly biblical. We have placed the
word 'sombre' in quotation marks, because we wish to
prevent this outlook from being identified with some form
of pessimism. The suffering is not an expected or unexpected
setback which troubles the outlook for the Kingdom, but
it is an unavoidable and recognizable indication of the

presence of this Kingdom on earth. That is why it is often spoken of in great soberness and in an undertone of deep joy. I mention only a few examples. From the sermon on the mount, 'Blessed are those who are persecuted for righteousness' sake, for theirs is the kingdom of heaven' (Matt. 5.10). From the first church history, 'Then they left the presence of the council, rejoicing that they were counted worthy to suffer dishonour for the name' (Acts 5.41). From Paul, 'We sent Timothy . . . to establish you in your faith and to exhort you, that no one be moved by these afflictions. You yourselves know that this is to be our lot' (I Thess. 3.2f.). From James, 'Count it all joy, my brethren, when you meet various trials' (James 1.2).

The reason for this attitude toward suffering is clear from other passages. Jesus prepares his own for suffering through the speeches, as recorded by Luke, during the Last Supper (they must sell everything, and buy a sword—the sword of Word and Spirit—which will keep them during the coming oppression), 'For I tell you that this scripture must be fulfilled in me, "And he was reckoned with transgressors" ' (Luke 22.37). John records the same in the farewell address as follows, 'If the world hates you, know that it has hated me before it hated you. . . . "A servant is not greater than his master." If they persecuted me, they will persecute you' (John 15.18-20). Peter's first letter puts it this way, 'But if when you do right and suffer for it you take it patiently, you have God's approval. For to this you have been called, because Christ also suffered for you, leaving you an example, that you should follow in his steps' (I Peter 2.20f.). This is probably what is meant by John's observation in his first letter (4.17), that we may be confident in the day of judgment, 'because as he is so are we in the world'. The well-known but often misunderstood words about bearing the cross must also be viewed in this light. Jesus talks about this in connection with the prophecy of his own suffering (Matt. 16.21-26), and of the conflict his appearance will let loose (Matt. 10.34-39). Jesus Christ, in whom the Kingdom took shape in this world, must in this encounter, which became a deadly struggle, take on the *Gestalt* of the crucified. And wherever his power is placed in this world, this same figure must make its appearance. It is an indication of the fact that it is really Christ whose power enters life. The Church, which is his body, does not escape the cross either, since this also was the case with the Head.

It is not surprising, then, that the whole concept of being Christian is viewed repeatedly in this light, especially by Paul. 'And if children, then heirs, heirs of God and fellow heirs with Christ, provided we suffer with him in order that we may also be glorified with him' (Rom. 8.17). We may not draw the romantic and narrow conclusion from this, that it is true always and everywhere of all Christians in the same degree. In Col. 1.24 Paul states, 'Now I rejoice in my sufferings for your sake, and in my flesh I complete what is lacking in Christ's afflictions for the sake of his body, that is, the church.' The afflictions Christ had to suffer continue in his body, the Church. The decisive, atoning work occurred in the suffering on the cross of Golgotha, but this did not yet complete the measure of the Kingdom's suffering in the world. The Church also represents her Lord to the world through her suffering. But not every member suffers in the same measure. During his imprisonment in Asia Minor Paul received the blows meant for the entire Church. When the congregations around him live in peace it is because the hate of the world falls on him as the substitute for all those Christians. He rejoices that in this way he removes a heavy burden from them. Today, too, there are persons, groups and churches in the body of Christ who serve as substitutes, and who, at the battle-front, receive blows on our behalf (missionaries, oppressed and young churches, etc.).

It is clear from all this that suffering is a vital part of the fellowship of Christ. It is also clear why the New Testament does not speak primarily of victory and balance of power. Behind all this there is no particular logic or world-view; primarily not even experience. Suffering as the lot of the Church follows from the fact that suffering was central in the life of Christ. A slave is, indeed, not above his master.

If Christ had to suffer defeat, and if the counterforces seemingly won the victory, then this will also be the calling of those who belong to him. The history which begins with the cross of Christ will repeatedly result in the cross.

Suffering in History

Suffering in the imitation of Christ is, of course, always a matter of the individual, but this individual suffers as a member of the Church. The Church suffers in the individual, and also often bears the suffering as a community. That is why suffering is essential in the history which begins where the Church comes into existence through the missionary enterprise. It is, therefore, not surprising that in those passages of the New Testament where the eyes are turned towards the introduction of the Kingdom into history, a dark picture of suffering as a fundamental factor in the process of the Kingdom of God is presented (e.g. Matt. 24; and Revelation). If I understand it correctly, the New Testament knows a threefold, closely connected situation in which the suffering of Christ is continued in the world—persecution, competitive doctrines of salvation, and apostasy.

Persecution actually begins immediately after the Church's arrival. The first half of Acts, especially, presents the opposition of legalistic Israel to the new Lord. The second half presents the opposition of the pagan forces, which are willing to give this new Lord a small place, but who at all cost want to withhold dominion from him. In I Peter and Revelation we see how the conflict with these forces must lead to persecution of the Church.

The *apostasy* presupposes another situation. It can take place only where the gospel has found roots in one form or another (Luke 8.13). This could occur in a small group of the Church's members, but it is clear that the apostolic words about the apostasy in the latter days, and certainly when they speak of 'the' apostasy in connection with the antichrist (II Thess. 2.3; I John 2.18; I Tim. 4.1ff.; II Tim. 3.1ff.), assume that the gospel is broadly and deeply rooted in the world. The apostasy as a historical force and historical process is a theocratic concept. This needs no particular argument after what has been demonstrated in the preceding chapter. Wherever the missionary enterprise has gone, it is unavoidable that sooner or later the now mature man will turn against his deliverer. Apostasy, however, is a negative concept. Eventually man cannot live by it. Apostasy demands a positive content. That is why even in the New Testament this concept is unnoticeably changed into that of *competitive doctrines of salvation*. I Tim. 4.1 is an example: 'Now the Spirit expressly says that in later times some will depart from the faith by giving heed to deceitful spirits and doctrines of demons.' 'False prophets' are often mentioned in this connection. It is clear that the man who rejects the salvation of Jesus Christ cannot exist without some form of salvation. He is negatively or positively under the influence of Christ's salvation to the extent that his own doctrine of salvation is greatly coloured by it. For examples of these competitive doctrines of salvation and their proponents see Matt. 24.5, 11, 23-26; I Tim. 4.1; II Peter 2; I John 4.1; and Jude 4.

When such a doctrine of salvation gains control over the life of a state it becomes a totalitarian ideology. This leads unavoidably to conflict with the Church. A new *persecution* will be the result. The persecution is in that case not caused by the opposition of the old forces against the new Lord. It now bears a typical post-Christian character because it stands against the background of apostasy and false messiahs. This is the way in which the persecution is described in the passages dealing with the antichrist. Although a sharp division has no value here, it is well to note that in the New Testament, persecution is on one hand a sign of the Kingdom's breakthrough into history, and on the other hand it marks a final phase of the Kingdom's elaboration.

If we translate this into the categories introduced in the preceding chapter, then the encounter between the gospel and a culture begins with the opposition of the old forces which characterized that particular culture. From the per-

secutions in the Roman Empire, through the resistance of
the German tribes, to, for instance, the Mau-Mau uprising,
history—especially the history of missions—has given many
examples of this. The antichristian revival of the great world-
religions, which is now taking place after the first period of
missions, must also be seen in this light.

Once the gospel has taken root in a culture, and the old
powers are more or less driven back, the phenomenon of
apostasy appears in the foreground. This has increasingly
been the case in Europe during the last three centuries.
Apostasy is the central *Gestalt* the suffering of Christ momentarily assumes among us. Sociologically, psychologically,
and historically much more could be said, of course, regarding the phenomenon which in a narrower sense is usually
called secularization. But all this receives perspective and
value only when one recognizes the theological necessity of
the apostasy. Only then will the Christian Church be able
to find her place in time without defeatism or frantic activism.
To be obligated to live and labour in a wilderness of indifference by people who think they know better can become
a heavy burden for both minister and congregation. We
should, however, 'not be surprised . . . as though something
strange were happening to you' (I Peter 4.12). The pressure
of post-Christian indifference is the burden of suffering now
placed upon the Church. She may consider it, too, an indication of the Kingdom's presence. She must respond to it with
the same soberness and joy as the early Church had done in
her situation.

But man cannot long endure the apostasy. Existence without a Lord and a purpose eventually leaves him cold and
lonely. A 'Nothing' comes into being which tries to change
the old powers into new forms. Neutral, secular existence,
which often lives on a mutual limitation and neutralization
of the powers, sometimes plunges itself recklessly into a new
mythical, sacred concept of life. Apostasy always carries
with it the possibility of a new competitive doctrine of salvation. Nietzsche was the prophet of both. 'Have you understood me? Dionysius against the Crucified . . .' (conclusion

of *Ecce Homo*). This competitive doctrine of salvation is often outwardly tolerant, although it may be coupled with a great inner pride, as is the case with many forms of syncretism. But it only sets the sphere of indifference and negation around the gospel on a higher plain. It is different when nihilism has undermined life to the extent that a new doctrine of salvation in the form of a restoration of the natural powers becomes a political necessity. It then comes in the form of a totalitarian ideology such as National Socialism and Communism. The only possible attitude they can take toward the Church is that of persecution. This situation is then not dissimilar to that which introduced the gospel into our culture. To be sure it is less possible for the post-Christian forces to give the impression of harmony which characterized it during its pre-Christian dominion. After Christ they were no longer a matter of course. Through their grimness, desperation, and craftiness they try to force themselves on man, proving how unnatural they have become, and how difficult it is for them to withdraw from the Kingdom's presence. They also face a much broader barrier—how different from in the beginning—namely a barrier of many who, although they are not Christian themselves, have tasted the humanity of the life secularized by Christ, and who do not wish to lose it. Thus, it is evident that the political doctrine of salvation with its persecution signifies an end, but not *the* end because it is again repelled in order to make room for a mutual limitation and neutralization of the powers, in which the suffering of the Church no longer bears the form of persecution, but that of apostasy and indifference.

We cannot neglect discussing *Islam* in this connection. Since we are untrained in this field we are unqualified to discuss this subject, but we can call upon many experts of the past and present who have struggled with what may perhaps be called the most puzzling phenomenon of world history. Islam is the greatest stumbling block on the road from Kingdom to history. At the same time Islam cannot exist without the Kingdom of Christ. Mohammed began with the thought of bringing the Judeo-Christian revelation to his own pagan people. All of Islam's notions find their origin in this revelation. Therefore Islam is principally different from the other great world religions which are forms of the dominion of the natural powers. But the idea of Revelation underwent a fundamental change in the hands of Mohammed. Revelation is changed into a natural religion, contrary to its own character, which keeps millions of people, who believe that they possess the 'higher', from an encounter with Christ. In the faith of his followers Mohammed began more and more to take on the appearance of the counter-christ. Islam is 'the pagan duplication of Jewish existence'.[1] 'Motivated by its Jewish and Christian inspiration Islam aspires to be a theocracy. The fall which took place at the outset of its course is the cause that it fundamentally represents a radical, worldly form of theocracy.'[2] 'In Islam man succeeded in turning Revelation into a "Religion".'[3] 'Post-Christianity can only be a contra-Christianity or an anti-Christianity. The throne of Christ, once it has been placed in the world, cannot remain unoccupied.'[4] In Islam we find the elements of Christ's historical suffering as they are presented in the New Testament. Islam is the great apostasy and competitive doctrine of salvation in one. Both are geographically expanded to the extent that an innumerable mass of people has been made inaccessible to the Lordship of Christ. Ethically and culturally, too, Islam is the greatest adversary of the gospel. It gives man the illusion of being delivered from paganism, without in the least giving him the freedom which comes through the appearance of Christ. Gospel and Islam belong together as the sun and shadow. Islam is *the* form in which the negative signs of Christ's presence take on world-historical proportions.

Repetition and Typology

Wherever Christ makes history through the missionary proclamation, the elements described above will raise their heads. They always differ due to the fact that it is impossible to repeat historical situations, but they are essentially the same because Christ and natural man do not change. Real history is, then, also characterized by repetition. That is why the boundaries between history and the times-without-history ostensibly disappear. For, as we have seen, repetition belongs to the latter. But although we must here use the same word, it does not carry the same meaning. Repetition in the times-without-history is the analogue and result of the repetition characteristic of the events of nature with its determined course of the seasons. Here, however, we are concerned with a repetition of encounters; a repetition which above all contains progress, and which presses on to a higher plain. This will become clear later.

The realization that the same situations and figures return repeatedly is a part of the Old Testament concept of history. This was already made clear in the second chapter where, among other things, we observed that Israel expected a repetition of the miraculous Exodus. The same is true of the New Testament. There events are described in terms of earlier events, especially those of the Old Testament. This is first true of the earthly history of Jesus himself. The forces of chaos which in the Old Testament opposed the dominion of Yahweh rise up again against him at the end of history. We have seen how Jesus saw his function in the midst of the beasts of Daniel 7. The Gospels and Epistles are full of the knowledge that the Old Testament situation repeats itself in and around Christ in a decisive manner. Matthew in particular frequently states that the Old Testament scriptures were being fulfilled in Jesus. Rachel's weeping was fulfilled in the children's murder (2.17). What God had prophesied to Isaiah as a result of his preaching was fulfilled in Israel's obduration regarding Jesus (13.14f.). The suffering of the innocent at the hands of his adversaries (the Psalms are full of his lamentations) was fulfilled in the suffering and death of Christ. Jesus' words on the cross are for the most part Old Testament quotations.

One often finds these passages to be confusing because the

word 'fulfil' is not understood to be connected with the
Messianic period and with the repetition motif. Take, for
instance, the strangest example, Matt. 2.17f. When Herod,
the enemy of God and his people, murdered the children of
Bethlehem, 'then was fulfilled what was spoken by the
prophet Jeremiah: "A voice was heard in Ramah, wailing
and loud lamentation, Rachel weeping for her children; she
refused to be consoled, because they were no more." ' This
is found in Jer. 31.15. There it concerns the lamentation
which arises when the Benjaminites are taken into exile.
Jeremiah sees in this a repetition of the tribal mother,
Rachel, who died in the neighbourhood of Bethlehem at
the birth of her son Benjamin. Jeremiah sees the repetition
of a situation which took place centuries earlier. In repeatedly different and yet repeatedly similar situations rises
the lamentation of God's suffering people. But Matthew
speaks of more than repetition; namely, fulfilment. All this
centuries-long suffering reaches its decisive zenith in Christ.
Anyone who states that Matthew was 'mistaken' because he
did not know the situation which caused Jeremiah to write
this only shows his own shallow understanding. He knew
better than we what Jeremiah meant. Like Jeremiah he
lived by the mystery of repetition; but unlike Jeremiah he
also lived by the mystery of fulfilment—the end of history.
That is why he was able to write as he did.

But Jesus Christ is not only the end of history; he is also
its beginning. For that reason he does not end the repetition
motif, but through the proclamation of his dominion it is
activated throughout the entire world. That is why for us,
too, the Old Testament motifs continue to express what is
essential in history. The New Testament is aware of this.
The 'abomination that makes desolate' from Dan. 12.11
returns in the history of the end (Matt. 24.15). Antiochus
Epiphanes rises again (compare Dan. 11.36 with II Thess.
2.4); the serpent from Genesis 3 (Rev. 12), the beasts of
Daniel (Rev. 13), and the great Babylon the Old Testament
prophets spoke about (Rev. 17), all return after—indeed
because of—the dominion of Christ, as the great adversaries

which he calls to life by his dominion. In Revelation they look exactly the same, and bear the same titles as they do in the Old Testament.

This repetition motif is common to the Old Testament, the New Testament, and the Rabbis. It is the expression of a common knowledge of the mystery of history. A typical example is the rabbinic history which states that Pharaoh was the only Egyptian who survived the crossing of the Red Sea, and who consecutively reigned as the king of Nineveh, the king of Babylon, Antiochus Epiphanes, and Titus (who destroyed Jerusalem). 'Until the end of the world he will bear a thousand names, for like Israel, Israel's enemy is eternal.'[5]

The modern reader who begins somewhat to understand this soon tends to characterize and dismiss this with the word 'allegory'. But that is a confusing misunderstanding. The biblical view of history is not allegorical, but typological, which is almost its opposite. The Hellenistic Jewish philosopher, Philo of Alexandria, was the master of allegory. Everything temporal is a parable to him, a symbol of that which is timeless and of an internal event: in other words, a symbol of the victory of man's higher spiritual faculties over the lower senses. This is how he reads his Old Testament. He views the Passover as the cleansing of the soul; in the Exodus he sees the exodus from the physical world to the spiritual, in which the lower passions (the Egyptians) are destroyed; he views the wandering in the wilderness as the journey of the soul to perfect illumination by the divine spirit; and so on.

Typology is completely different. It does not think in terms of timelessness, but entirely in terms of history. For here the external is not a parable of the internal, but the earlier is a parable of the later, or better, the historical is like the Historical. Allegory looks inward, into the soul. Typology looks ahead, into history. That is, typology looks back into the past and there finds the key to the present and future in the encounters between God and the world.

The interpretations which Christians in the course of

111

centuries have given to contemporary history must be seen against this background. They repeatedly saw the beasts of Daniel and the biblical Babylon take on new forms in Diocletian, Mohammed, the Pope, the Turks, the Enlightenment, Liberalism, Hitler, and Stalin. Thus, through the experience of their own time they sought to understand the biblical mystery of history in which the suffering of Christ progresses in constantly new repetitions. We can criticize these interpretations only when we recognize this. Criticism can move in three directions.

1. No thought was given to the possibilities, limitations, and authority of such interpretations. We wish to discuss this in the last chapter.

2. The localization of the antichristian power was often too one-sided and too absolute in *one* particular appearance. By doing this the proponents became blind to changes in that appearance, and to other antichristian appearances, especially those in their own camp.

3. They often saw in those appearances the antichrist himself already present as the zenith of evil in the last days. This exaggeration and anticipation would not have happened in a proper conception of the antichrist, or in a broader understanding of history.

But all this does not remove the fact that wherever Christ arrives the counterforces are awakened, and the believers are called to share in the struggle and suffering that fact brings with it, and to determine their place in it. In the course of the centuries the Christian Church has not been able to determine, and cannot determine her place without a certain measure of interpretation. That these were wrong in the eyes of later generations or contemporaries who had a different interpretation, should not lead to the conclusion that one can live without interpretation and (as a consequence of it) decision. He who does that no longer lives.

However, if this is not to lead to Christian pharisaism because we are inclined to place the antichristian forces with the 'others', then we must realize that the struggle between Christ and the antichristian forces, which is the theme of history, is not the same as the struggle between faith and unbelief. The matter then becomes too subjective. Christ's Kingdom is more than his members' disposition of faith. And the kingdom of the adversaries is more than the unbelievers' notions. The greatest antichristian power is precisely the wild wheat, the weeds from Matt. 13.24ff., the pseudo-church. Christ has been harmed more by disobedience, and by what seemed to be faith, than by the world's fiercest attacks. Conversely, Christ also uses men who have no faith in him, but who in one way or another have dedicated themselves to the task he champions. We shall return to this in the next chapter.

The Antichrist

History is not only repetition. It also contains progress. In their repetition the motifs aim for higher ground in order eventually to reach a high-point and turning-point. In this, too, history is nothing less than a repetition of events around Jesus Christ which have reached cosmic proportions. The Gospels remind us of the increasing opposition called up by Jesus, of the circle of enemies which narrows itself around him, of the power of evil which culminated in Judas' betrayal. Jesus uses the image of growth (also for evil) in the parable of the two kinds of seed (Matt. 13.24ff.), and in the synoptic apocalypse (Matt. 24.32-44). Growth is essential for every historical process. And wherever the missionary endeavour arrives, the weeds are sown and begin to grow.

The process of growth stands graphically before us in the Gospel narrative. It does not have the same clarity in the broad field of cultural history. The New Testament does not attempt to demonstrate this clarity historically. But our attention is purposely directed to the end of this process of growth, to the culmination of the evil forces which were loosed by Christ, which received form in what we, along with I John 2.18, call the 'antichrist'. It is a new name, but the expectation is that of the Old Testament as we noted in the second chapter. The figure of Gog in Ezekiel 38 and 39, who just prior to the time of salvation unites his forces against God and Israel, is to be viewed as an antichrist. The idea of a concentration of evil is more clearly expressed by the small horn of Dan. 7.8 and in the description of the king in Dan. 11.36. These texts also inspired the New Testament writers. While the title 'antichrist' appears only in I John, we can find the figure in more than one tradition. Paul discusses him in II Thess. 2.3-12. In Revelation he appears as the analogue of the 'beast from the sea' from Daniel 7 (Rev. 13.1-10). He is mentioned twice in I John (2.18; 4.3). He is missing only in the synoptic tradition. But even the synoptists know of a future culmination of the antichristian forces as the 'abomination that makes desolate' (Dan. 12.11); they know that false Christs will arise and that there will be a great persecution which will cause many to fall and which will kill the love of the majority (Matt. 24 and par.). In the New Testament we deal with different variations of a common theme which must have occupied a central place in the faith of the primitive Church. Paul is surprised that the young congregation at Thessalonica has taken no account of the antichrist in their expectation. He writes, 'Do you not remember that when I was still with you I told you this?' (II Thess. 2.5). This sounds strange to us, unless we remember that the mystery of history is the same as the mystery of Christ, and that Paul and his congregation lived under the influence of the fact that the world only recently crucified the Lord of glory. With this in mind it is important to note that the title 'son of perdition' occurs twice in the New Testament; once in connection with Judas (John 17.12), and once in connection with the antichrist (II Thess. 2.3). Just as in the decisive battle against Jesus, Satan entered into Judas, so also in the last round of the cosmic struggle the power from the abyss will again be embodied in a person.

The title 'antichrist' originated in earliest Christian tradition, and is a good characterization of the figure they wished to describe. The meaning of 'anti' is 'in the place of' and 'against'. The antichrist is not separated from Christ. Without Christ he is absolutely unthinkable, he is bound to Christ and must attest Christ's dominion also in that he exists by fighting against everything Christ means in the world. He is at the same time Christ's competitor and caricature who contests Salvation by replacing it with his own salvation. This is emphasized by the context in which he appears in the Revelation. He is the product of the dragon, the old serpent, Satan, who has been called God's ape. The beast from the sea was sent by the dragon as the Father sent the Son. The beast from the earth (Rev. 13.11-17) accompanies the beast from the sea in order to win man to his dominion, in the same way the Spirit realizes the Son's work in man. The antichrist is the demonic reflection of the Son in the pattern of a trinity made up of the dragon and the two beasts.

The antichrist, then, cannot originate in paganism, but only in a becoming Christian de-Christianized world. 'The' apostasy (II Thess. 2.3) is the condition for his arrival. He is preceded by many antichrists—apostates—who went out from the Church because they were not a part of her (I John 2.18f.). The antichrist is the organic end-product of a becoming Christian de-Christianized world. This concept is quite essential to the witness of the New Testament (II Thess. 2.3, 7; I John 2.18; 4.3; Rev. 13 as result of Rev. 12). And all three of the characteristics of Christ's suffering in a becoming Christian world—apostasy, competitive doctrines of salvation, and persecution—at their fiercest extremes seem to be characteristic of the antichrist's advent.

The great apostasy is no more a return to paganism than it orginates in paganism. This is impossible because Christianization has forever closed the way back to it. It is worthy to note that the New Testament witnesses were aware of this also. For would it not have been natural for them to suppose the antichrist to be the great representative of paganism whom they saw around them and who threatened young Christianity? Yet, the antichrist is not described as a religious figure, but radically atheistic, in accordance with

Dan. 11.36f.: 'He shall exalt himself and magnify himself above every god.' He who rejects the God and Father of Jesus Christ can, after the unmasking of the gods affected by Jesus, move only towards a religious nihilism which sees in everything that is called god a projection of the human 'I', and in this way keeps but one god—projecting man who now takes his projections back and becomes proudly aware of the burden of his autonomy. Man is hardly able to bear this loneliness, however. But the antichrist becomes man's substitution, taking the burden upon himself and in this way giving man the opportunity to fall back on religion in the sense that he now can worship the antichrist as a deified man. That is why he is called the one 'who opposes and exalts himself against every so-called god or object of worship, so that he takes his seat in the temple of God, proclaiming himself to be God' (II Thess. 2.4).

Paul follows this in verse 5 with the words, 'Do you not remember that when I was still with you I told you this?' This is an interesting question when we keep in mind that the church at Thessalonica still needed to be fed with milk, and that in our established churches the antichrist is hardly ever—let alone 'oftimes'[6]—mentioned! The image of the antichrist with its atheistic and even anti-theistic religiosity was apparently an essential element in early Christian faith in which history as the activity of God played a much greater part than is generally the case with us. A reading of Revelation 13 will lead us to the same conclusion. There the beast from the sea also originates in apostasy; that is, from the reaction to the appearance of the child and the woman in Revelation 12. There, too, it is the bearer of religious nihilism which is four times described with the Greek word for 'blasphemy' (vss. 1, 5, 6). And there also the other side of this blasphemy is the fact that the beast himself becomes the object of worship. This, according to Rev. 13.11-17, is organized by another beast who rises from the earth, and who, as the competitor and imitator of the Holy Spirit, represents the lying power of propaganda. This obviously leads to the persecution of the real believers.

This concept presupposes that the antichrist is expected as a political totalitarian power which, in agreement with the planetary extent of Christ's reign, possesses a universal world-rule at the end of history. This is also clear from Paul and Revelation. The beast of Revelation 13 is a combination of the four beasts in Daniel which represent political powers. And verses 16 and 17 mention a complete economic boycott of the adversaries which is not possible without political power; while in Revelation 17 the antichrist as beast is combined with the woman who is seated on it, and who is called 'the great Babylon' (vs. 5), the Jewish title for godless political power.

Here the question tends to rise whether the antichrist is a person or a group, a tendency or a spirit of the age. Whenever this is viewed as an 'either-or', we are trying to force biblical thought into a Western alternative. Christ is a person, and at the same time he is the head of a body (moreover, he himself is this body, I Cor. 12.12) who with his Spirit moves triumphantly through the world; the antichrist is similar to all this. The beast from the earth is placed beside him in order to point out what a strange and far-reaching influence will be placed on the mind. But this does not take away the fact (it rather assumes it) that the centre of all this is a person. He is more than a group; he is the object of this group's worship, and that can only be a person. The texts cannot be understood without this assumption. The world becomes more dependent on a few domineering personalities in the measure that individuality is submerged. The mass and the strong personality belong together. The Word could work only, and was able to conquer and influence only, after it had become flesh (for only the person can bear power). In the same manner the demonic power will become flesh and person.

The question inevitably arises whether something more concrete can be said about this mysterious person. In view of II Thessalonians 2 we must leave it unanswered. It is clear that Paul was not thinking of a contemporary, but that it is a future figure. Every attempt to identify him with a historical person is expressly discouraged (vss. 3, 6, 8). The whole matter stands or falls with the certainty that Jesus cannot yet return, because the antichrist has not yet arrived. When Paul describes him to some extent, it is only because he quotes and expands what he has read about it in Daniel. In Revelation the matter seems to be somewhat different. We know that the apocalyptists and rabbis considered the Roman Empire as the fourth beast of Daniel. They, too, use 'Babylon' as a pseudonym for Rome. And when in addition to this it mentions (Rev. 17.9) that the great Babylon sits on seven heads, i.e. seven hills, everyone's mind must have been drawn to the seven hills of Rome.

It seems clear that when Revelation discusses the antichrist it refers to the Roman Empire. This led many to seek for a particular emperor behind the beast from the sea, usually Nero. When one wishes to pursue this line of thinking, however, it seems to run into nothing. At first glance the opposite is the case. Many then point to the mysterious, repeated expression that one of the beasts' heads was fatally wounded, but that his fatal wound healed (13.3, 12, 14). This is offered in connection with the rumour that the hated Nero, who committed suicide in AD 68, was not dead, but that he would reappear in the East with a large army. This explanation is appealing, but improbable. This brief rumour, which was not fulfilled and soon disappeared, could never have become the occasion for characterizing the beast from the sea. The key for this mysterious expression must be sought not in an uncertain historical context but in the context of exegesis and salvation history. The fatal wound received by the adversary was caused by Christ himself. Chapter 13 may not be separated from chapter 12. The dragon had a universal reign before Christ's coming. But only after Christ's birth does the dragon really come to life (12.3), and through Christ's victory the dragon is cast out of heaven (vss. 8, 9) with the result that he explodes into 'great wrath' because 'he knows that his time is short' (vs. 12). Through all this he unsuccessfully tries to destroy the woman in the desert (vss. 13-18) in order from that moment to continue his great struggle through the new concentration of his power, the beast from the sea. The dragon gave him his own power, his throne, and his great might (13.2). Immediately after this the fatal but healed wound on one of the beast's heads is mentioned. One could say that the actually destroyed might of the dragon relives in this beast.

What causes this might to relive? It is not the worship the beast from the earth has tempted man to perform (13.15-17). This is result, not cause. The cause is described in chapter 12. The loss of his legitimacy brings the dragon to angry activity. Christ's power which defeats him drives him to develop his impotent might (12.12). Through the fatal blow which he himself inflicted, Jesus Christ lays the foundation for the resurrection of the dragon's power. In this way the dragon, and subsequently the beast, have become the great adversary and caricature of Christ who through a fatal blow inflicted at the crucifixion gained the victory. The beast with its seven heads and fatal wound is the caricatured reflection of the slain Lamb which is the Lion of Judah with his seven horns and seven eyes (5.5f.). This caricature presents a fundamental difference (which is essential to the caricature): the defeat of the Lamb is visible, and his victory is hidden, while with the beast these things are reversed.

With this in mind it is possible to say something about 17.8, 'The beast that you saw was, and is not . . . and the dwellers on earth . . . will marvel to behold the beast, because it was and is not and is to come.' This has nothing to do with Nero's disappearance and expected reappearance. One must remember what was said of God-Christ in 1.8, 'who is and who was and who is to come'. His caricature was (before Christ's coming), is not (through Christ's victory), but he unites his impotent might so that he will be for a short time.

We are inclined to view the most mysterious and most discussed mark of the antichrist—the number 666—in this light. Whoever believes that a particular Roman emperor is signified must deal with the so-called number value of letters. This leads to dozens of different explanations which are almost all possible, a few probable, but not one satisfactory. It seems more relevant to consider here the symbolical meaning of numbers in Revelation (3, 4, 7, 12, 1,000, 144,000 or 12 × 12 × 1,000). Seven is the number of divine and also of satanic fulness. A number which contains three sixes reminds us of the six working days; a symbol of man's highest development of power outside the sabbath of God's work. Like the other mysterious expressions it speaks of the enormous power within the actual impotence which is the mark of the antichrist.

Thus, the antichrist of Revelation is Rome and not Rome. We are placed before a phenomenon which is already known to us from the Old Testament and which is typical of a biblical understanding of history. Rome is partially the appearance of the future antichrist. The antichrist will repeat and increase what was done by Roman emperors such as Nero and Domitian. The end time can best be approached in terms borrowed from the dark present. In that way the present is illuminated for what it is before God, and the contours of the end time become visible in the writer's own time. It must be noticed that the allusions to the writer's own time are relatively few, and that the terms are usually of the kind belonging to general salvation history, i.e. real in all times. For that reason it is impossible to know whether the writer of Revelation believed the antichrist to be a Roman emperor, or whether he believed that the emperor only foreshadowed the antichrist in the spirit of I John 2.18. It is even possible that this question was considered unimportant by him.

The last mark of the antichrist we wish to point out is the limited time allotted to his work and power. It is not often realized how essential this is. The dragon knows 'that his time is short' (12.12). His great creation, the antichrist, is given forty-two months, that is, three and a half years, half of seven. If fulness and completion are expressed by the number seven, three and a half must mean that his life and work will be broken half-way through their course. His labour remains incomplete. The same image is presented in chapter 17. The beast 'is to ascend from the bottomless pit and go to perdition' (vs. 8), as though in the same breath. The terrible seventh head is allowed to remain for only a short time (vs. 10), and the ten horns receive power for only one hour (vs. 12). II Thessalonians 2 states the same thing. The 'restrainer' is described (vss. 6f.), after which follows the statement, 'and then the lawless one will be revealed, and the Lord Jesus will slay him with the breath of his mouth and destroy him by his appearing and his coming' (vs. 8). Here, too, rising and setting are mentioned in the same breath. For a moment the antichrist appears on the stage only to be chased away. For he exists through an impotent power.

The background of all this is the fact that the antichrist is only the shadow of Christ. He is fettered to his great Master like a slave. Without him he can do nothing. And whatever he does is a witness to Christ's victory. For the antichrist is the union of the adversaries which were called to life by the Kingdom of Christ, and are not able to overcome this Kingdom, but against their own will are, through their negativity, a witness and affirmation of this Kingdom in order soon to be permanently defeated by it.

NOTES

[1] A. Th. van Leeuwen, 'Islam en Jodendom', *Wending* XI, 5-6, 1956, p. 290.

[2] H. Kraemer, *De Islam als Godsdienstig- en als Zendingsprobleem*, The Hague, 1938, p. 12.

[3] E. Kellerhals, *Der Islam*, Basel, 1945, p. 377.

[4] *Ibid.*, p. 372.

[5] I found this reference in Paul S. Minear, 'The Wounded Beast', *Journal of Biblical Literature* LXXII, 2, 1953, p. 101.

[6] The word 'oftimes' does not appear in either KJV or RSV. The author's Dutch version apparently has it. [*Trans.*]

7

THE RISEN CHRIST IN HISTORY

We have been delivered from nature by the birth of Jesus like the child Moses from the crocodiles in the Nile, and we have been handed over to the Spirit and to history like Moses to his sister Miriam. If man would stop gazing and staring like the donkey by the manger, he would realize that he has been placed in a storm of the Spirit, and that God's wonder is the element of his life.

O. Noordmans, *Gestalte en Geest*, Amsterdam, 1955, p. 81.

WE HAVE seen that the suffering of Christ, his cause, and his Church (these are inseparable, but not identical) is essential for mankind which has been marked by the reality of the Kingdom. But this cannot be the last word regarding that reality since Christ not only suffered and was crucified, but he also arose and was glorified, and now lives as the victor over all that opposes him. This could not be neglected in the preceding chapter. We now wish to examine more closely the positive side of his reign.

The Power of Christ's Resurrection

Cross and resurrection are not active in the same history-making manner. This is connected with their different place and function in salvation history. The cross is central to the history of our old guilty world which died with the erection of the cross. For that reason the suffering and death of Jesus are vividly described in the Gospels, in much detail and in concrete terms. It is different with the resurrection. It is the breakthrough of God's new world which is radically different from the old. What really happened is not told, cannot be told. And the outstanding reaction of the first witnesses is fear and alarm. After his resurrection Christ is entirely different from what he was before, he is hardly or with difficulty recognized. The result of all this is that the Gospel narratives about the resurrection are much shorter than those about the passion. This is not because the first was considered of less importance. On the contrary, the opposite is true. But in our terms nothing more can be said. There are no words to describe this unique event. The resurrected Christ is the firstfruit. Those who are Christ's come after him, namely, in his future. His passion immediately continues in the world, but the natural conclusion of the resurrection is future. The difference between cross and resurrection is the difference between present and future. This is clear in Paul's thinking about these facts of salvation. 'For if we *have been* united with him in death like his, we *shall* certainly *be* united with him in a resurrection like his. . . . But if we *have died* with Christ, we believe that we *shall* also live with him' (Rom. 6.5, 8). 'Provided we suffer with him in order that we may also be glorified with him' (Rom. 8.17). 'Becoming like him in his death, that if possible I may attain the resurrection from the dead' (Phil. 3.10f.). The cross continues to the present; the fruit of the resurrection is waiting for us in God's future.

Yet, this is only a half-truth. In the first and third passages cited above the other half of the truth is already clearly expressed. 'We were buried therefore with him by baptism into death, so that as Christ was raised from the dead by the glory of the Father, we too *might walk in newness of life*' (Rom. 6.4). 'That I may know him and *the power of his resurrection*, and may share his sufferings' (Phil. 3.10a). In this respect, II Cor. 4.7ff. is particularly clear. Paul discusses the death aspects and the resurrection aspects of his ministry. 'We are afflicted in every way, but not crushed; perplexed, but not driven to despair; persecuted, but not forsaken; struck down, but not destroyed; always carrying in the body the death of Jesus, *so that the life of Jesus may also be manifested in our bodies*' (II Cor. 4.8-10). 'For as we share abundantly in Christ's sufferings, *so through Christ we share abundantly in comfort too*' (II Cor. 1.5). If we bear in mind Paul and John's words about being more than conquerors, about faith that overcomes the world, and so much more, then we must say not only that according to the New Testament the elaboration of the resurrection is future, but also that a 'small beginning' (*Heidelberg Catechism*, answer 114) of this becomes visible in this life and this old world.

It would be very strange if it were otherwise. Christ was resurrected not outside of, but in this world. During the forty days his resurrection receives a certain, although strange and incidental, extensiveness and form in our old existence. It is the resurrected One who says to us, 'I am with you all your days.' It is the glorified One who sends his Spirit to the world. Suffering, as we have seen, is the indication that Christ has become history's hidden point of reference. It is not pointless suffering; it is the mark of his victory. That is why there is a certain ray of resurrection light in the Gospel narratives about the suffering (the transfiguration on the mountain, the soldiers' falling down, the fact that Pilate finds him innocent, the inscription above the cross, the Roman captain's witness, the veil which tore in two, and the appearance of the dead). The power-filled life of the believer is an analogue of this which can be reasoned away by outsiders, but which he himself believes and experiences. The Acts of the Apostles, the Epistles, and, following these, twenty centuries of church history are witnesses to this fact.

The Resurrection in History

What is true of Christ's suffering is also true of the power of his resurrection. This power manifests itself not only in the individual, but also in the Church as a whole. As such it is of constitutional significance for the Kingdom and its history-making. The first and central mark of this is the continuation of the missionary enterprise (Matt. 24.14). This fact is without parallel in history. Faith in Christ seems to find root in all races and cultures, and in every defeat finds new power for its continuance. In comparison with the resources of the political powers it is a miracle that there is any progress in the face of shortages of manpower, money, and influence. The word 'miracle' is used in its full biblical sense as a mark of the Kingdom. We have become so accustomed to it that we walk amidst the miracles without seeing.

The New Testament is full of a tense expectation and an unshakable certainty that this dispensation before the consummation (since and through the advent of Christ) will unveil itself as analogous with his victory. If we view the New Testament in this light, we will find in Jesus' own words various statements which have reference to the future *growth* of his work. Most obvious are the parables of the mustard seed (Matt. 13.31f.) and of the leaven (Matt. 13.33). In the past these were too generally interpreted as 'the expansion of God's Kingdom'. A reaction followed which saw the point of similarity not in growth, but in the contrast between the small beginning in the present and the great result in the consummation. The latter is, of course, correct, but it is not in contradiction with the first. The transition from small to large is purposely described not as a sudden change, but as growth. The image of growth appears repeatedly in Jesus' words and parables. One cannot assume that this is irrelevant. The reaction was followed by a counter-reaction which rightly places the emphasis on the fact that it concerns the outward and inward growth of the Church.

In this connection we are also reminded of Jesus' statement regarding the great harvest and the too few labourers (Matt. 9.37ff.). This is worked out in greater detail in the beautiful passage where Jesus describes the fields as white and ready for harvest (John 4.35-38). Notice the triumphant sound of Jesus' words in Luke when he tells that the seventy return, that Jesus sees Satan fall from heaven like lightning, that he rejoices in the Spirit because the time of salvation has arrived in which all things are delivered up to him and are revealed to the children (Luke 10.17-24). Elsewhere the *durability* of Christ's work is in the foreground (Matt. 16.18), and still elsewhere we are repeatedly directed to the *signs* which follow the apostles and the Church—the expulsion of demons, the works of the Spirit, and the healings. All of this does not remove the fact that the opposition is strong. But there is a *restraining power* which makes certain that the witnesses need not seek for words (Matt. 10.19), and that when total defeat threatens total victory makes its entrance (Matt. 10.23). Wherever the opposition is not restrained God reveals his reign in the fact that he *reverses* the opposing power in order to serve his plan. Christ's cross is the greatest proof of this. This certainty is clearly expressed in Acts 4.24-28 when the Church confesses in her prayer that although the pagans and nations rage, they 'do whatever thy hand and thy plan had predestined to take place'.

In Acts, also, the concept of *growth* appears constantly in connection with God's Word (6.7; 12.24; 19.20; 16.5). But it receives greatest emphasis in the Letters to the Ephesians and Colossians. The building of the Church grows into a holy temple (Eph. 2.21), or from Christ the body 'grows with a growth that is from God' (Col. 2.19). The meaning of this is that 'we all attain . . . to mature manhood, to the measure of the stature of the fulness of Christ', in order 'to grow up in every way into him who is the head' (Eph. 4.13-16), or, that we cause all things to grow unto him. This growth of the body which builds itself up in love comes from the head.

These expressions are usually entirely, or at least primarily, interpreted to mean the progress and sanctification of the individual members of Christ's Church. Without denying the latter, we must ask whether that is all there is to it. These passages clearly deal, not with the individual, but with the Church as a whole. In the preceding chapter we noticed in the discussion of Col. 1.24 that Paul presupposes a certain measure of suffering which is to be 'filled' by the Church. In the passages mentioned above it concerns a measure of growth in Christ's fulness. We do not fully comprehend the meaning of these words when we fail to

appreciate their dimensions of salvation history and eschatology, and when we forget their cosmic implications which
are so clearly presented in the Ephesian and Colossian
epistles. There is powerful growth in the body of Christ.
This is connected with God's plan not only to provide a
head of the Church, but also to unite all things in Christ as
the head (Eph. 1.10, 22). It is not clear from these mysterious words how Paul imagines this to take place. That the
tiny congregations of Palestine, Asia-Minor, and Greece
were to be seen in this light must have been a great matter
of faith for him which could be maintained only with the
eye focused on the glorified Lord.

The book of Revelation deserves our special attention in
this respect, for it is repeatedly read as the key witness for
a one-sided, dark picture of history. There is reason for this,
of course. But if after reading a man remembers primarily
the terrible judgments predicted in this book, he has not
understood its main point. This main point is the fact of the
certainty that the resurrected Jesus Christ now has all
power on earth, and that nothing escapes his almighty love.
The vision of history (chapter 5) begins with the Lamb's
opening the book of history. This means not only that he
explains it, but also that he introduces the end of history,
and that he is its beginning and end. This motif rules all
that follows. The opening of the seals (chapter 6) brings
calamities and persecutions. But these proceed from the
Lamb. This cannot be said, however, in a strict sense of the
word, because the evil forces often seem to take the initiative. For that reason the characteristic words 'power *was
given* him (them)' are used. Nowhere is the initiative taken
away from God and the Lamb. For even chaos can be
understood only as a result of the Lamb's wrath (6.17).
The events are also set in motion and led by the prayers
of the saints (8.3ff.). It is no wonder, then, that every stage
of history is accompanied by *songs of praise* in heaven.

That it is really God-in-Christ who is behind the judgments seems obvious from the manner in which the judgments are always *restrained*. The oil and wine are not harmed

(6.6), only a third of the world is destroyed (8.7ff.; 9.15) and that with the intention that two-thirds might repent (9.20). Those who are sealed, the 144,000 and the un-numbered crowd, are kept safe through it all (9.4). In chapter 11 this restraining power is particularly evident in the form of the two witnesses who perform their work un-disturbed for three and a half years. The antichrist replaces their work by *his* three and a half years, but their death is followed by a rapture which moves man deeply and which gives honour to God. The child escapes in chapter 12, and the woman is protected in the desert for three and a half years which is obviously the period of the two witnesses ended by the beast from the sea. We discussed 13 in the pre-ceding chapter. Chapter 14 again sounds the songs of praise followed by a threat for the enemies and an en-couragement for God's children, and it closes with a view of the coming judgment. Only with the description of the 'seven plagues' in chapters 15 and 16 (on the analogy of the plagues in Egypt) does everything seem to become darkness. But this too is from beginning to end a proclamation of God's superior power over his enemies whose chastening is meant to lead them to salvation. Chapters 17 and 18 describe in great joy the fall of the great adversary, Babylon. From this moment on the tone steadily becomes *more triumphant*, and is only temporarily broken by the rise of Gog and Magog (20.7-10) who are immediately defeated, which is the signal for the arrival of the heavenly Jerusalem.

More than any other book, Revelation is a witness to the power of the resurrected Christ over the world. This may even be believed when it seems that God is no longer in control of things, and that the cross of Christ is all that remains. The message of Revelation is that God's Kingdom is active in our midst through suffering and judgment, re-straint, and triumph.

The Restrainer

With these witnesses in mind we are somewhat prepared

to examine Paul's mysterious words concerning 'the restrainer'. In II Thessalonians 2, the important exposition of Paul's theology of history which we have discussed previously, we read after the announcement of the antichrist the following words, 'And you know what is restraining him now so that he may be revealed in his time. For the mystery of lawlessness is already at work; only he who now restrains it will do so until he is out of the way' (vss. 6f.). Until the present these strange words have given interpreters much discussion. It concerns something that restrains (vs. 6) or someone who restrains (vs. 7). The Greek is most faithfully translated when we read: 'he or that which suppresses'. What is this power which suppresses the antichristian forces? There are dozens of interpretations. Not all of these are worthy of serious study, so we limit ourselves to the most important.

A large group of interpreters, particularly among the church Fathers but stretching through into the present, believe that Paul had the *Roman state* in mind (Tertullian, Lactantius, Chrysostom, Luther, and Stauffer). Some of them thought of a particular state officer such as Claudius, Vitellius, Vespasian, Titus, or Trajan, and a few thought of Nero's honourable tutor, Seneca. We must not look in that direction, however. Paul is not trying to present a private opinion about the relationship between the Christian Church and the political constellation, but he is consciously unfolding the Christian confession concerning history. The 'suppressor' must be a reality in direct connection with God's saving activities in the world. This cannot be said of the Roman state or one of its representatives. There certainly is no basis for saying that Paul expected the great adversary of the antichrist from the Roman state; on the contrary, he expected the antichrist to be a head of state.

Others point to the contrast between the suppressor and the 'lawlessness', and consider the first as the power of the *law*, either in the sense of a general order of law (e.g. Zahn), or in the sense of the gift of common grace. Or they believe that the suppressor is the binding of the law on man, or a

Christian authority. But these explanations, too, fail to recognize the close connection between the suppressor and Christ. The lawlessness is not a general concept, but it expresses the rebellion against Christ's authority.

Still others believe it is the *angelic power*. This seems more strained than it really is. For did we not notice in the preceding chapter that Paul borrowed the terms for his description of the antichrist from Daniel? In Daniel we read that certain good or evil angels, called 'kings', battle against the progress of God's saving activity (Dan. 10.13, 21; 12.1). One of the most important of these is the king of Israel, the angel Michael. In certain papyri Michael is called the 'suppressor', a name which in pagan circles is ascribed to the Egyptian god Horus (see the *Poimandres*). There is some basis for saying that Paul and his readers took this notion from Daniel, although this is most uncertain, since Michael's role receives little mention, as does his relationship to the antichrist. Pointing to Daniel is clearly not satisfactory, since Paul views angels never merely as supernatural, mythical powers, but always in connection with the realities of earthly life. Thus, the important question still is, 'What earthly reality did Paul here have in mind?'

When we must think of a force placed here by God in his saving activities we come close to the conclusion of those interpreters who believed the suppressor to be *the proclamation of the gospel* (Theodore of Mopsuestia, Theodoret, Calvin, and Cullmann). This explanation is closest in agreement with the fundamental structure of the biblical concept of history, as it began to appear in the preceding chapters. It offers a parallel with such expressions as 'the gospel must first be preached to all nations' (Mark 13.10ff.; Matt. 28.18; Acts 1.7), and with Paul's argument in Rom. 11.13ff.: namely, that the preaching of the gospel which is in close connection with Israel's rejection, precedes and to some degree postpones the consummation. It is possible that the first figure from Revelation 6, the rider on the white horse, agrees with this same insight. The glorious progress of the gospel restrains the eschatological sufferings. One question deserves careful consideration: Does the vagueness of the suppressor lead us to the necessity of describing him in still broader terms, and not only to think in terms of the missionary proclamation, but more generally of the dispensation of the Holy Spirit and of his work in the missionary endeavour, the building up of the Church, and the Christianizing forces of the gospel in general? (That is why we can think with Cullmann particularly of Paul's own person and work.) In this we also find a good explanation of the variation between 'the suppressor' and 'that which suppresses'. The personal points to God and his Spirit, the neuter to his activities. It may seem strange that it speaks about the removal of this suppressing force. However, we find a clear parallel in Revelation 11 in which the two witnesses are the restrainers whose work is replaced by the short activity of the antichrist. We cannot say that their work is interrupted, because the antichrist will come 'when they have finished their testimony' (11.7). God is not surprised or made powerless by this, he only suspends the work of his Spirit in order momentarily to give the godless forces a chance for development.

A statement about the suppressor ('you know what is restraining him now') is like a floating iceberg. Only a small part is visible, but by the manner of the wording we know that we are dealing with a fundamental and deep-rooted article of faith in the earliest Church. Christ's resurrection power was to them a tangible reality in history, in a way which we can hardly imagine now. They lived by the fact that although the gospel of Christ was everywhere opposed, and that it brought suffering and persecution, the adversary cannot reach his objective since Christ truly arose in this world. The enmity Christ's work necessarily called to life is thus suppressed with a powerful hand. Faith and experience are not contrasting elements in this. This insight originates in faith in the resurrected Christ, but it is affirmed by the work of the Holy Spirit in the Church's growth and in the irreversible progress of the gospel proclamation.

Christ the Meaning of History

Repetition and Typology

In the preceding chapter we saw that new analogies to the crucified Christ repeatedly take place, and history can be understood in this way only via the so-called typological method. This is also true of Christ's resurrection. On the one hand Christ's delivering appearance means the fulfilment of the positive signs in the Old Testament, and on the other hand this fulfilment means the foundation for a new series of analogies, particularly where the missionary proclamation changes the face of the world.

In connection with the negative signs we paused momentarily at the manner in which Matthew uses the word 'fulfil' with the infants' murder at Bethlehem (2.17f.). This is immediately preceded by the story of the escape to Egypt followed by the words 'and [Joseph] remained there until the death of Herod. This was to fulfil what the Lord had spoken by the prophet, "Out of Egypt have I called my son" ' (2.15). We must exclude the possibility that Matthew was ignorant of the fact that these words from Hos. 11.1 concerned Israel's Exodus from Egypt under Moses. Fulfilment here means that whatever God wanted to accomplish in the Exodus was attained in the delivering appearance of Christ. Christ's coming fulfilled not only the deliverance from Egypt, but also that from Babylon, as John the Baptist asserts (Luke 3.4f.; Matt. 4.15f.). Indeed, all the marks of God's superiority over the opposition of the nations and the sin of his people are fulfilled in Jesus—the brass serpent, the manna, the rock which produced water, etc.

But this fulfilment at the same time means a new beginning. God's triumph in Christ's resurrection finds new analogues in the now-present end time: analogues which again can be described in Old Testament terms. Ps. 110.1 was a much cited text in the primitive Church. 'The LORD says to my lord: "Sit at my right hand, till I make your enemies your footstool." ' This humiliation of the enemies is already visible in the signs of the outpouring of the Holy Spirit (Acts 2.34f.) and it continues until finally death is cancelled (I Cor. 15.25ff.). The healings reveal that the stone rejected by the builders has become the head of the corner (Acts 4.11) and this is even more evident in the Church's growth (Eph. 2.20). The great work mentioned in Hab. 1.5 repeats itself in the missionary endeavour. What Ps. 8.6 claims about man—'thou hast put all things under his feet'—is already true of the resurrected Christ (I Cor. 15.27; Eph. 1.22; Heb. 2.5ff.), and becomes especially visible in the building up of the Church. In the midst of the tensions of history the delivered Church adopts Moses' song after the crossing of the Red Sea (Rev. 15.3) and the power of Moses and Elijah against God's enemies returns in the two witnesses (Rev. 11.6).

That is why Christians during the course of the centuries have been permitted and even commanded to seek and find traces of the resurrected Christ in the events of contemporary history. (See the final chapter for the necessity and dangers of such interpretations.) It is a noticeable fact that far fewer indications of Christ's glory have been sought and found than is true of Christ's cross. Yet, these are by no means missing. Eusebius of Caesarea saw them in the conversion of Constantine and the subsequent end of the persecution of Christians. These signs were later seen in the Christianization of the German tribes, in the kingdom of Charlemagne, in the unified culture of the Middle Ages, in the Spirit's mighty workings during the Reformation, in the revival movements and missionary enterprises of the last two centuries; Blumhardt saw them in the signs of healing and conversion, and so on. The Church cannot find its place in the world without seeing, or at least the desire to see, these signs. Faith does not depend on vision, but it does lead to vision. For faith, among other things, means the certainty that wherever Christ is glorified in this world and reigns over this world, his resurrection power is active in history, and as such takes on form, i.e. it becomes visible. Visibility does not always mean recognition, and it never means recognition without faith. But wherever this visibility is believed, recognition is automatically sought.

The Future Sign—Israel's Conversion

In the preceding chapter we saw that the antichristian forces developed to a maximum in history. The question arises whether there is a parallel of this in the case of the power of the resurrected Christ. It is possible to believe that the answer must be negative. In the history before the consummation the resurrection is hidden more than the cross. The cross is elaborated and worked out entirely in this dispensation. The elaboration of the resurrection is itself the consummation. Thus this popular Christian interpretation of these things leads to a pessimistic view of history. If in contradiction to this we present the opinion that we may also expect an elaboration of the resurrection into a maximal power in this dispensation—in so far as this is possible in a sinful world subject to death—we present this not from a different view of history, but from the facts presented by the New Testament witness.

What does it really contain? The New Testament's surprising and yet, after close examination, obvious answer is *Israel's salvation.* Israel's repudiation of her calling in rejecting Jesus Christ is the great abnormality of history. If it is true that the rejected king of Israel is risen and that that resurrection is elaborated not only in individual lives, but also in history, then that nation for whom he primarily came, and which before any other is reserved for his glory and service, that nation which died to its calling in the death of Jesus, will have to find its way back to its calling through Jesus' resurrection. If there is such a thing as a suppressing power, then it will find its crowning in the suppression of the great force which at one time tried to suppress Jesus. And if the end of history will be a cosmic analogy to and expansion of the cross and resurrection, then Israel may perhaps crucify her king anew (many believe that the antichrist will come from Israel); but more than this, Christ will be resurrected in Israel, and this nation will be resurrected in him. In the victory over the great scandal in history—Israel's disobedience—the power of the resurrection will become evident, or it will not become evident at all. The faithfulness and sovereignty of God are at stake. Here as nowhere else his faithfulness will prove to go beyond and overcome our unfaithfulness. This is true according to the witness of both the Old and the New Testaments. 'For the gifts and the call of God are irrevocable' (Rom. 11.29). 'What will their acceptance mean but life from the dead?' (Rom. 11.15).

Israel's Future According to the Old Testament

Since this expectation is far from universal in the Christian Church we shall describe and prove the above more closely. The Old Testament presents little difficulty in this task. The final salvation of the world is there dependent on the expected glorification of Israel under her Messiah. Israel's blessing includes the blessing for all other nations (Gen. 12.3). In the end time the two great hostile world powers, Egypt and Assyria, will make peace through Israel's mediation (Isa. 19.23-25), the heathen will then go to the holy mountain to learn God's revelation (Isa. 2 and Micah 4), and they will be considered to have been born in Zion (Psalm 87). However differently the time of salvation may be described, it was obvious to all the prophets that Israel will then be the focal point of the world.

But can Israel not fall and squander away her promised privileges by breaking the covenant with God? Indeed, Israel can and did fall. The prophets abound with this terrible possibility and reality. Together with God's grace she then loses the land in which God allowed her to live. She is scattered among the nations. As sure as this is, it is even more certain in the minds of the prophets and the prophetic community (by the latter I think particularly of Deuteronomy) that this could never be God's final word. 'A remnant returns', and that remnant grows into the new, real Israel God has in mind. There is only one reason for this amazing return—God's faithfulness to the nation with whom he began, and his maintenance of the covenant in spite of the nation's unfaithfulness. One may read this put in strong words such as those of Isa. 54.9; Jer. 16.14f.; 30.11; 31.35f.; Amos 9.8; Zech. 10.6. It will dawn on Israel in wonder. Before this occurs she must follow long detours of guilt, and go through deep valleys. Most of the relevant words may seem to have been fulfilled in the Babylonian exile. But Ezekiel and Zechariah, who already were able to think and live by what happened after the exile, saw much darkness before them. Ezekiel saw the arrival of Gog (Ezek. 38 and 39, see chapter two of this book), and Deutero-Zechariah saw Israel's transgression against the one sent by God followed by a new siege and destruction of Jerusalem. These last prophecies reach far beyond the history the prophet himself experienced. We see here the conviction that Israel's guilt will continually prove to be great and will be punished, but that God's faithfulness will prove greater and will not rest until Israel shall blossom as the sanctified focal point of a happy world. The last word concerning Israel is not spoken by the unfaithful nation herself, but by Yahweh who remains true to his covenant.

Israel's Future According to the New Testament

These matters seem to be more difficult in the New Testament. The opinion is often given that Israel fulfilled its calling in the world by producing Christ. And by crucifying him she once and for all determined her lot, and her significance in salvation history is gone for ever. Israelites do have the opportunity for conversion, but only individually like the pagans. The Church, built out of individuals, has taken Israel's place.

This opinion is at first glance rather plausible. Christ is the end of history. The Kingdom arrived in him, the wall of partition between Israel and the pagans is removed, and the gospel makes its way from Israel into the world. In this great change the primary attention is focused on the new man which makes his appearance and the new relationships which are created. Israel's positive significance is then less obvious. Because Israel crucified her Messiah all the emphasis concerning Israel falls on the negative role she played in the great change. Again, as in the days of the major prophets, but in a stronger degree, Israel is disobedient to her calling and calls judgment upon herself. Jerusalem is destroyed and the people are scattered among the nations. The Gentiles enter into the full light of the gospel, and at the same time Israel as a nation enters into the darkness of rejection. Everything seems to point to the fact that the Old Testament expectation concerning Israel's central and positive role in the Messianic era has been repudiated by the facts, or at best has found a fulfilment which the prophets neither desired nor expected.

On closer examination, however, the picture changes. In the first place Jesus is Israel's Messiah and King. Luke, the evangelist to the Gentiles, says that God 'will give to him the throne of his father David, and he will reign over the house of Jacob for ever' (1.32f.). The shepherds are told that the Messiah's birth means joy 'to all the people', that is, to all Israel (2.10). Simeon praises the child not only as 'a light for revelation to the Gentiles', but also 'for glory to thy people Israel' (2.32). Jesus' own appearance was in agreement with this. He has not himself broken down the wall between Israel and the nations. His task was to reveal himself to Israel as the promised Messiah in order that Israel, knowing that the Messianic age had arrived, would present this message to the world. For that reason the apostles, who must call Israel to recognition of her Messiah, must limit themselves to Israel and were not allowed to go into Samaria (Matt. 10.5f.), and Jesus in originally refusing to help the Canaanite woman appealed to the fact that he was sent to the lost sheep of the house of Israel (Matt. 15.24). This unwillingness of Jesus has often given readers much difficulty. He seems so pitiless. But this unwillingness becomes understandable when we realize that Jesus maintains the order which the prophets expressed for the end time: the Messiah will appear, Israel will gather around the Messiah, and then

Israel will become a focal point and light for the Gentiles.

But it steadily becomes clearer that things take a different turn, and that Jesus, in this respect also, as the end is as well the new beginning of history. For Israel does not recognize her Messiah and is, therefore, not able to fulfil her calling in the end time. That is why the vineyard will be given to others (Matt. 21.33ff.) and the originally invited guests of the coming feast are excluded (Matt. 22.1ff.). In itself it would be possible for the consummation to come without Israel, since Israel excludes herself through her own fault. This is not how the matter lies in the New Testament. Jesus weeps over Jerusalem, and the book of Acts is the account of one great but fruitless attempt still to win Israel for her calling. This points to the fact that Israel's attitude is a matter of grave importance. For the holy order of the Messianic age has been disturbed by the Messiah's rejection (even though this disturbance is, according to Deutero-Zechariah, not an unforeseen surprise to Israel's God). In the early chapters of Acts the disturbance seems again to be settled. Pentecost is a feast clearly within Israel. At that time Peter makes a strong appeal to Israel to recognize her Messiah. 'For the promise is to you and to your children and to all that are far off, every one whom the Lord our God calls to him' (Acts 2.39). Note the order! Later it follows, 'God, having raised up his servant, sent him to you first, to bless you in turning every one of you from your wickedness' (3.26). Three thousand let themselves be baptized on the day of Pentecost, and during the following days and weeks this number rapidly increased.

Will the time of salvation continue? Peter insists, 'Repent therefore, and turn again, that your sins may be blotted out, that times of refreshing may come from the presence of the Lord, and that he may send the Christ appointed for you, Jesus, whom heaven must receive until the time for establishing all that God spoke by the mouth of his holy prophets from of old' (3.19-21). What strange words! Here is said nothing less than that the return of the Messiah and the arrival of the time of salvation promised by the prophets, the times of refreshing (or revival), depend on Israel's acceptance of her Messiah. For a moment it seems that this will indeed take place. Mighty workings of the Spirit occur, as a parallel to Jesus' first successes in Galilee; healings, miraculous punishments, even quickening of the dead, and a liberality in giving which clears away poverty. But as was true in Jesus' life, hate and opposition grow. The apostles, and later Stephen, are persecuted. Israel as a whole again chooses against her Messiah. The miraculous time of salvation recedes. At the same time we note that the Samaritans and the Gentiles come flocking—Simon the magician, the Ethiopian eunuch, and Cornelius. They do not come via Israel, but in spite of Israel, through the mediation of the small remnant which is Israel's substitute in achieving her destiny. The Messiah's course repeats itself again, not in Palestine, but in the lands of the Gentiles. Paul goes to Asia and Greece. Everywhere he goes he begins his preaching in the synagogues, for he, too, is called as a witness to Israel (Acts 9.15). Sometimes he receives their attention temporarily. But the synagogues as a group reject him. Now again the Gentiles come flocking without Israel. Acts ends by describing that this was also Paul's experience in the capital of the Empire. His last recorded words are directed to the Jews of that city, 'Let it be known to you then that this salvation of God has been sent to the Gentiles; they will listen' (28.28). Since then Israel is no longer considered as the bearer, but as the adversary, of salvation. There are, of course, many Israelites in the Church—the eschatological reality in which Israel and the nations encounter one another in their praise of God and his Anointed—but in comparison their number constantly becomes smaller. The Church is becoming a fellowship of Gentiles. Israel's privileges and decrees are transferred to them and seem no longer to apply to Israel.

But there is absolutely no truth in the latter. No matter how far Israel drifted from God's calling, the faith of the prophets continues to live in the New Testament. This faith was that Israel's unfaithfulness can never cancel God's faith-

fulness, and that Israel will yet take a central place among
the nations in the work of salvation. There is a difference
of emphasis at this point between the Old and New Testaments, but no more. In the Old Testament God's faithfulness stands in the foreground, but it is stated that this is not
a guarantee that the people will not sin, or that they will
not be led through God's dark detours. In the New Testament, Israel's disobedience and blindness are in the foreground, but it is stated that nevertheless this cannot frustrate
God's faithfulness to and salvation plans for his people.
When Jesus discusses Israel's judgment this certainty sounds
through, 'Behold, your house is forsaken and desolate. For
I tell you, you will not see me again, until you say, "Blessed
is he who comes in the name of the Lord" ' (Matt. 23.38f.).
'Jerusalem will be trodden down by the Gentiles, until the
times of the Gentiles are fulfilled' (Luke 21.24). One must
not say that these are 'only' two texts. The fact that these
things are formulated with almost no emphasis (all emphasis
falls on the first part, the judgment of punishment) speaks
volumes. These are expressions of what was for Israel, on
the basis of the Old Testament promises, a divine matter-of-
fact. Earlier in this chapter we made use of the image of the
iceberg. It may be used here too. Only two texts of the
words of Jesus are visible above the water level, but we
know the entire iceberg from the Old Testament prophetic
writings. Of course Israel will come to her Messiah, this is
what the earliest Palestinian congregation confessed, for
God's promises made in the Scriptures are sure.

In the chapter 'Jesus Christ the Beginning of History' we
discussed the problem of *Naherwartung*. We then also touched
upon the fall and acceptance of Israel. We must now say that
the manner in which this matter in the New Testament is in
agreement with the Old Testament, proves again that the
Naherwartung in the usual sense must have been foreign to
early Christianity. The fulness of the Kingdom could not
come as long as Israel persisted in her rejection of the
Messiah. The question concerning *Naherwartung* as a matter
of doubt and argument could only arise when the Gentile-

Christian Church believed that it had crowded Israel out of her place.

Romans 9-11

Paul's rich train of thought about Israel in Romans 9-11 is rightly understood against this background. It then becomes clear that his expectation regarding Israel was more than a personal hobby which in his case as a Jew can be completely explained by psychology. He presents the faith of the Lord himself and of the earliest congregation, and in his own way brings a connection between this faith and the painful experience of Israel's apostasy. This passage is not an eccentric outburst, nor is it particularly difficult as is suggested by the contradictory explanations. It becomes difficult when one wishes it to say something it clearly does not say. Paul begins by saying that he reduces the fall of Israel to the same impenetrable and sovereign decree as that which at one time lifted the patriarchs and the nation from paganism (chapter 9). This decree, however, is not completely hidden. Paul sees light on this from three directions. 1. This decree is not arbitrary; it corresponds with Israel's unwillingness to walk God's way of salvation (9.31-33; 10). 2. Due to this decree the Gentiles have been drawn to the light (9.23-30; 10.19f.). 3. Israel is not completely forsaken by God; the 'remnant' which the prophets saw enter into the Messianic age through this crisis became a reality in the Jewish-Christian Church. Paul had in mind the great crisis of the Messiah's appearance, death, and resurrection. The remnant which lives through this crisis and recognizes Jesus as the Messiah is the real Israel. That it is only a small group need not cause confusion. For Israel is not merely a biological entity, but here the biological and spiritual go together. 'For not all who are descended from Israel belong to Israel.' Israel lives out of a correlation between promise and faith (Rom. 9.6ff., 27, 29; 11.5-10).

Many readers prevent further insight into Paul's argument because they stop here, and the later ideas of chapter 11

which reach beyond this they wish to press forcefully into
the form of the preceding. But Paul progresses because he
knows that God progresses to overtake previous actions by
new actions. That Israel is rejected through her own fault,
that only a remnant will be saved, and that Israel is included in this remnant in a spiritual sense, does not alter
the fact that these are not God's last words. In 11.11 things
take a new twist for which the preceding has not prepared
us. Paul here presents a two-sided discovery.

First: Israel cannot deny her calling in the end time
through her disobedience. She is and remains the link
between the Messiah and the nations. She could be this link
through her obedience, but even now, in her *dis*obedience
she still fulfils her functions as a link. For (the narrative in
Acts proves this) it is through rejection on the part of the
synagogue that salvation reaches the Gentiles. A direct
route to Christ is made for the nations through Israel's
stepping aside. 'Through their trespass salvation has come
to the Gentiles' (11.11; see also 11.24).

Second: 'Now if their trespass means riches for the world,
and if their failure means riches for the Gentiles, how much
more will their full inclusion mean!' (11.12). That is, one
day the remnant will grow to include the whole of Israel.
This impenetrable decree by which Israel was first elected
and later rejected, is for this concrete, natural, carnal
Israel in the deepest sense a decree of *grace*. All Israel will
be saved (11.26). There is only one reason for this twist, 'As
regards election they are beloved for the sake of their forefathers. For the gifts and the call of God are irrevocable'
(11.28f.). Paul ends with the same impenetrable decree
with which he began; only now the shudder is replaced by
the song of praise: 'O the depth of the riches and wisdom
and knowledge of God!' (11.33-36).

This impressive train of thought is clearly and entirely
in agreement with the way in which the prophets discuss
Israel's unfaithfulness and God's faithfulness. The manner
in which Paul uses the word 'remnant' is perhaps the only
new thing. With him it seems to have not an exclusive, but

an inclusive meaning. The remnant is the foundation and the guarantee for a new future in which all Israel will be saved. 'The remnant will grow to completion. As such it is a productive number, not an unalterable minority.'[1] The reason for this is that for the prophets the remnant was an eschatological entity, and for Paul, now that the future had arrived, it was a historical entity. For him the end is at the same time a new beginning. It is questionable, however, that this inclusive meaning of the remnant was foreign to the prophets. The remnant of Isa. 10.20-23 returns in Isaiah 11, where the Messiah is like a 'shoot from the stump' which grows mighty and gathers the scattered Israel to itself as a focal point of the nations.

Doubtless some questions remain, especially in Rom. 11.11-36. This is inherent in the matter. When the perspectives are so wide, the details become somewhat dim, and we cannot expect to describe everything we see as though it were written in the land registry or attested by a lawyer. It seems strange, however, that on the basis of this experience interpreters conclude that nothing of importance is to be seen! Allow me to point out a few of these difficulties.

1. What is the meaning of the word 'fulness' in verses 12 and 25 [RSV reads 'full inclusion' in vs. 12, and 'full number' in vs. 25—*Trans.*]? First must 'the full number of the Gentiles come in' (25), then Israel too after a period of 'failure' comes to 'full inclusion' (12). In this way the two texts can be connected. It is then still not certain that 'fulness' in both cases has the same meaning. In verse 12 it is paralleled by 'too short', according to the translation by the Netherlands Bible Society ['failure' in RSV—*Trans.*]. This suggests that both words have a quantitative meaning. Here, then, 'fulness' means 'full number' in contrast to the small remnant of Paul's day. 'Fulness' is then the same as 'all Israel' in verse 25. The best translation would be 'becoming full in number'. Others translate it as 'falling short', namely, concerning justification by faith. This fits in well with 'failure'. Then 'fulness' is their fulfilment of God's will, or their full participation in grace. Linguistically and rhetoric-

ally this translation is a little far-fetched, and we must choose the first as more appropriate. Does 'fulness' in verse 25 mean 'the full number of the Gentiles'? In itself this could be possible. But in the context Paul does not allow the same broad perspectives for the Gentiles as he does for Israel. To think of the full number of the elect is not in line with the argument either. Others have defended a qualitative explanation. They believe that the Gentile-Christian Church must undergo 'a condition of ripening and of full growth into life', and through this call Israel to emulation. 'And so' (26), namely through emulation, Israel will be driven into the Church and to her destiny. This is not impossible; yet this explanation seems to go too far beyond the words of the text for ready acceptance. Without making a choice I would point to a third possibility. Nestle's edition of the Greek text in Rom. 11.25 points to Luke 21.24 which was discussed earlier: 'Jerusalem will be trodden down by the Gentiles, until the times of the Gentiles are fulfilled.' Parallel to this we might translate (Rom. 11.25), 'a hardening has come upon part of Israel, until the fulness of the times of the Gentiles has come'. This translation is unusual, but not at all impossible. It is completely in agreement with the prophetic proclamation. Israel's acceptance is preceded by the moment in which God puts an end to the dispersion among and the oppression by the Gentiles. The objection, however, is that the word 'Gentiles' in Romans 9-11 always means the 'Gentile Christians' (9.24, 30; 11.12f.). Perhaps we must in both texts accept the simpler translation of 'full number', although this leaves the meaning of verse 25 uncertain.

2. Rom. 11.15 reads, 'For if their rejection means the reconciliation of the world, what will their acceptance mean but *life from the dead?*' These last words allow for several interpretations. One could understand this to mean that Israel, having been converted, will become *the* nation of the apostolate, by which the world will experience a real resurrection in the spiritual, missionary sense of the word. But this spiritual meaning of 'life from the dead' is foreign to

biblical language. The expression is usually of an eschatological nature. That is why many read here that Israel's conversion is the immediate presage of the Kingdom of glory.

A third possibility is that Israel's road is here seen as an analogy and parallel to the road of her Messiah: Christ's rejection has a power of reconciliation; thus, the rejection of Israel has a reconciliatory effect, and the future path of Israel will also be analogous with Christ's resurrection.

There is, however, still a fourth possibility which deserves careful consideration: namely, that Paul says here that when God again turns to this nation, it means the re-establishment of Israel as God's people. For this re-establishment is presented in Ezekiel 37 in the figure of life from the dead. 'Thus says the Lord GOD: Behold, I will open your graves, and raise you from your graves, O my people; and I will bring you home into the land of Israel. . . . And I will put my Spirit within you, and you shall live, and I will place you in your own land' (Ezek. 37.12, 14, which follows the vision of 1-10). In my opinion Paul's words are at least an allusion to Ezekiel 37. This does not necessarily exclude that Paul, according to the second understanding, expected Israel's acceptance as God's last step towards the consummation.

3. What is the meaning of 'and so' in Rom. 11.26? We do not read 'then' or 'after this'. But there is no reason to exclude the possibility that this 'and so' is a future event. Paul is dealing with the historical order of God's activities, and only just before used the conjunction 'until' (25). Yet, 'and so' implies more than 'until'. However, it is less clear what the antecedent of 'and so' is. One could say: 'because the Gentile-Christian Church, which has come to full bloom, called Israel to emulation' (Grolle and others). One could also read: 'and so Israel is saved so that the last are the first, and the first are temporarily the last'. One could connect 'and so' with the result and the manner in which Israel will be saved, described in the words, 'The Redeemer will come forth from Zion', and so on. There is a combina-

tion of the last two possibilities in Barth.[2] I should like to describe 'and so' as: by means of the strange detour presented in verse 25.

4. Finally: What is meant by 'all Israel' which, according to verse 26, will be saved? Those who find difficulty with the strong emphasis on Israel's future salvation in this chapter, readily suggest that these words cannot be interpreted literally. It is impossible that all Jews, without exception, will one day come to Christ. Even if this were possible there would still be the preceding numberless generations who lived and died without Christ. Thus, they conclude, this expression should not be expanded beyond the fact that in a new or far future a large number of Jews will be converted. This conclusion is perhaps numerically correct, but it is Western and individualistic, and as such misses Paul's amazement and joy. It is a matter here not of the salvation of the individual but of the activities of God in history. Then the acceptance, although involving only the last generation, means the acceptance of Israel in all generations, a certain indication that as enemies of the gospel they were still at the same time beloved for the sake of the forefathers. And as Paul could not know what the numerical proportion in the last generation would be, so neither do we. Together with him we may say that it will be such that no one will be able to say that a great number of Jews are converted, but that all Israel is saved, Israel as a whole. He who would question this can never say that Israel is now hardened, seeing that at all times, there have been many Christian Jews. One can make it unnecessarily difficult for oneself. The moment will come that even the shrewdest exegete will feel some of Paul's joy, because (in a manner we cannot now imagine) all Israel will be saved.

These difficulties prove what has been stated earlier: that the main lines of Paul's argument in Romans 9-11 are clear. It is in complete agreement with the Old Testament and with what we found elsewhere in the New Testament.

People and Country

We are not yet finished with our subject. For we can never speak about the nation of Israel without mentioning the country to which God has connected this people in his saving activity. This will sound strange to many Christians. It is difficult for us to imagine that God's salvation activity is also concerned with geography. But things cannot be otherwise. God's actions take place amidst concrete, human existence which occurs not only in time and history, but also in geographic space. We all take this fact into account, when we talk about Canaan, Babylon, Jerusalem, Bethehem, Nazareth, Golgotha, the Mount of Olives, and so on. The question which concerns us here is whether God's future plan has to do with the land of Palestine, or whether it can be conceived apart from this. There is no doubt that in the Old Testament the people of Israel and the land of Canaan belong together, not by accident in the sense that all people must have a place to live, but by God's promise in which *this* people is connected to *this* land. Thus, we read in Genesis 12, 'Go from your country . . . to the land that I will show you. And I will make of you a great nation' (vss. 1f.). This move to Canaan is usually explained by the idolatry of Mesopotamia from which Abraham was to separate himself. In that case one forgets that Canaan was just as idolatrous. The entire Old Testament is full of temptations to Baal worship and to compromise with paganism which repeatedly led Israel astray. There must therefore be deeper and more positive reasons for the choice of this land. It is constantly called 'a land flowing with milk and honey'. The book of Deuteronomy could bear the title: Ode in Praise of the Land. It ends and culminates in the climactic moment in which Moses, just prior to his death, was allowed to see the whole land, 'a land which the LORD your God cares for; the eyes of the LORD your God are always upon it, from the beginning of the year to the end of the year' (11.12). Nothing is explained by these references, of course. But it is clear that in the Old Testament Canaan had a

147

place of great importance, which it received from the fact that God in his salvation activity has reserved this land for his people.

If this country is the indication of God's acceptance—even itself part of the content of this acceptance—then it is not surprising to read that the great sign—even the content—of God's rejection of his people is the break in the connection between people and country. And because Israel is no longer Israel without this country in which God has placed it, it is equal to saying that Israel's place in salvation has been removed. This, too, is a recurring conviction in the Old Testament, and it is especially central to Jeremiah and Ezekiel. I further draw attention to Lev. 26.31-35 and Deut. 28.64-66 as strong expressions of the place taken in God's judgment by the country, or rather the expulsion from the land in the dispersion among the nations.

Since God's judgment is not the last word but is followed by a new acceptance of grace, it is clear that this takes the form of Israel's return to Canaan. This, too, is for Jewish prophecy a divine matter-of-fact. I mention Deut. 30.1-10; Isa. 11.11f.; 14.1; 27.12f.; 35.1, 10; 43.5f.; 49.22; 62.4-7; 66.18-20; Jer. 16.14f.; 31.8-12; 32.36f.; Ezek. 36.8-12, 24, 28, 33-36; Amos 9.11-15; Zech. 8; 10.9f. Two quotations will make clear how closely connected people and country are in the eschatological salvation. 'I will plant them upon their land, and they shall never again be plucked up out of the land which I have given them, says the LORD your God' (Amos 9.15). 'You shall no more be termed Forsaken, and your land shall no more be termed Desolate; but you shall be called My delight is in her, and your land Married' (Isa. 62.4).

It is not possible to date all these expressions. Most of them are certainly connected with the Babylonian captivity and the return. However, wherever the origin of this connection between land and people—directly in the heart of Israel's relationship with God—it is quite possible that these prophetic utterances were also expressed when such historical circumstances were not present. At any rate it is obvious that the related texts from Zechariah were written long after the captivity. The prophet saw Israel fall into new sin and idolatry, and knew that this would again lead to separation of land and people. But beyond that he saw the appearance of a new union. The Dispersion is the repeated mark of God's judgment, and the return to the land is the mark of God's grace.

The question might arise whether the return follows the conversion of the people or *vice versa*. Sometimes one has the impression that it is the first, as in Deuteronomy 30, and sometimes the second, as perhaps in Isaiah 11, and certainly in Ezek. 36-37.14. In fact Ezek. 37.1-14 is very concrete and precise. Ezekiel sees Israel return. The scattered bones gather together again, 'but there was no breath in them'. After this the Spirit brings life to them through the prophetic word.

Before we leave the Old Testament proclamation concerning the country, we have still to discuss the question of why God particularly gave this small country such a highly strategic position. The question seems strange and impossible to answer. From our point of view it perhaps might just as well have been Thailand, Guatemala, or Lithuania. Of course, the choice of this particular country is centred in God's sovereignty. Palestine could have remained as unimportant as Syria or Amman. This does not mean that sovereignty is arbitrary. All of God's activities are characterized by a reasonableness of the highest order in which we firmly believe, and which we can sometimes see with faith's eye. The knowledge of God's sovereignty does not exclude but includes calling Canaan 'the most glorious of all lands' in the Old Testament (Ezek. 20.6, 15), and comparing it with Egypt as a land which needs no irrigation, but is fruitful of itself (Deut. 11.10-12). The title 'centre' of the earth (literally, 'navel') is significant (Ezek. 38.12, see also 5.5). One could here think of national pride and see parallels in China, France, and Britain. But the context points in the direction of Israel's defencelessness rather than pride. It concerns the attack on Israel by Gog. When

Rev. 20.7-10 again takes up this expectation, it is stated that the people of Gog and Magog rise from the four winds and surround the holy city. Both descriptions accentuate the fact that Jerusalem and Canaan are the centre of the earth. This seems insignificant. But it could have deep meaning. Throughout the civilized world, we count time from the birth of Christ. Perhaps this chronological fact has a geographic parallel in the remarkable fact that Canaan is supposed to be the division between East and West; between the two great intellectual structures of the world. At any rate it is more than a geographical accident. In the eyes of Westerners, Jewish biblical thought is Eastern: expressing itself in imagery, not in concepts. And in the eyes of the Easterners, it is Western because it demythologizes and secularizes the world. Perhaps this partly explains God's geographic strategy. Israel must live on the line of demarcation, on the navel. That is why Jerusalem cannot be in Belgium or Pakistan.

But now the New Testament! The question of the theological significance of the country is more strongly debated than that of Israel's future. The tendency is to say that the former has disappeared since now the whole earth has become God's country. Many love to point to Jerusalem's destruction as the sign that the role of Canaan has been completed. But when one reads Jesus' words about this against their Old Testament background, one is led to just the opposite conclusion!

We do not usually deal with Jesus' words about the future destruction of Jerusalem. Many read these as an indication of Jesus' supernatural insight into the future and as such they are considered as divine information. Others view them as partly or entirely unauthentic, as prediction after the event, and as such mere human information. In reality these words must be read as a continuation of the Old Testament prophecy of judgment. Now that Israel has rejected her Messiah and in that way has broken the covenant as never before, God will again break the connection between land and people, as earlier in the Babylonian captivity.

With the prophets this was never mere information. In the first place, it was a last call to repentance, spoken from the conviction that if this call were unheeded, the destruction of Jerusalem and the dispersion of Israel would be unavoidable. This is how we must read Jesus' words too. Their Old Testament background is clear in Luke 21.22, 'For these are days of vengeance, to fulfil all that is written.' Nestle notes (in his edition of the Greek New Testament) that 'days of vengeance' is an allusion to Deut. 32.35; Hos. 9.7; Jer. 5.29. Their content is an allusion to the whole prophecy of Israel's dispersion. But we have noted that this prophecy is not the last. The last of the prophetic proclamations is the certainty that no matter how large the detours, land and people will be reunited and Israel will reach its destiny in Canaan. The sole but sufficient reason for that hope is the faithfulness of God. Whenever Jesus discussed Jerusalem's destruction, it was for him—even as earlier for Jeremiah and Ezekiel—the penultimate and not the last thing that could be said about Israel and her country. We need not discuss this for it is clearly expressed in this connection: 'Jerusalem will be trodden down by the Gentiles, until the times of the Gentiles are fulfilled' (Luke 21.24). There comes a time, seemingly within this dispensation, in which God's faithfulness will triumph over the unfaithfulness of his people, and Israel will realize her destiny, in Palestine, as the great witness of God's salvation activity in the world. The question whether the return precedes the conversion or *vice versa*, cannot be answered. Nor is it clear how long this period of Israel's recovery is to be, and in what way Israel will fulfil her calling. This is hidden by the mists of the future. It will then be clear. Speculations may be attractive and inspiring, but they have no authority. It is enough to know that God's apparent humiliation at the hands of Israel will be changed into the triumph of God's faithfulness. This faithfulness has already in this dispensation revealed itself in Christ's resurrection to be sufficiently powerful over all that may resist it.[3]

The State of Israel

It is impossible to end this discussion of Israel's future without mentioning the state of Israel. Long before there was the slightest chance of Israel's return to Palestine this was accepted as a near and sure fact by the so-called chiliasts and sects. It is a strange experience for modern readers to see this fact described in books from the last century, often with the addition that Israel will return to Palestine unconverted. These surprising facts again set our thinking in motion, although they may not lead us to speak of the modern state of Israel in romantic and speculative terms. This nation, however, is at least a presage of God's future dealings with his people. Perhaps it is no more than a presage which will disappear like a *fata morgana* with a change in the political atmosphere. Perhaps it is more than a presage, and is already the actual beginning of God's new dealings with his people. In any case, it is not more than a beginning. A conversion of Israel to Christ is still out of the question. Israel's growing sympathy for Jesus of Nazareth may prepare the way for this, but could also mean that Israel is now further removed from him than during the generations which hated him. But apart from this central point, Israel herself is hardly aware of what has taken place since 1948. The majority views it in national, if not nationalistic, terms. The question what the connection between country and people means for God is in fact not asked. The result is that the great majority of Jews, who still live outside Palestine, are not forced to a clear decision with regard to the state of Israel. In the opinion of many it is still only a debatable project for winning and recovering land in the country which the Jews at one time possessed. It is more or less accidental, more or less right. One can accept it, or reject it. Most Jews by far still remain on the outside. So far as religion is concerned, the matter is from all angles still ambiguous. It is, however, not acceptable to believe that this will be true very long. However and wherever Israel appears it tends to be a stumbling block and the object of excitement for the nations. At any rate, with the surprising geographical and political fact of the establishment of the state of Israel, the moment has come for us to begin to watch for political and geographical elements in God's activities, which we have not wanted to do in our Western dualism, docetism, and spiritualism.

The Millennial Kingdom

At this point we must discuss another expression of the belief in future indications of Christ's sovereignty in history. This sign is the millennial kingdom, also called the kingdom of peace, or the intermediate kingdom because it falls between our dispensation and the consummation. We purposely deal with this subject after Israel's restoration. There are two reasons for this. In the first place, there is only one passage in the Scriptures (Rev. 20.1-6) which expressly and in detail discusses a future time of salvation within this dispensation, while the testimony concerning Israel's restoration, as we have seen, is heard more often and more strongly. In the second place, both subjects are so closely connected that the restoration of Israel guides our thinking to a future kingdom of peace. For no matter how close this restoration is thought to be to the consummation, it will take place in our space and time, and in our world it will take on a form and that a deep-moving and beneficial, revolutionary one. If a millennium is coming, then we know at least this, that a recovered Israel will be the centre of it (see Rev. 20.7-9). We do not know much more, as will become obvious. We can deal with these questions only as a result of Israel's restoration, and as a part of the circle of questions we just discussed. Whoever does not respect this order of proclamation and faith is in danger of isolating this confession of the kingdom of peace and bringing it suspiciously close to a faith in Valhalla or a fool's paradise. Since this has often been the case throughout church history, this confession has come under great suspicion from which it can be saved only by placing it in its proper context.

Let us begin by writing out the passage in question, Rev. 20.1-6:

> Then I saw an angel coming down from heaven, holding in his hand the key of the bottomless pit and a great chain. And he seized the dragon, that ancient serpent, who is the Devil and Satan, and bound him for a thousand years, and threw him into the pit, and shut it and sealed it over him, that he should deceive the nations no more, till the thousand years were ended. After that he must be loosed for a little while.
> Then I saw thrones, and seated on them were those to whom judgment was committed. Also I saw the souls of those who had been beheaded for their testimony to Jesus and for the word of God, and who had not worshipped the beast or its image and had not received its mark on their foreheads or their hands. They came to life, and reigned with Christ a thousand years. The rest of the dead did not come to life until the thousand years were ended. This is the first resurrection. Blessed and holy is he who shares in the first resurrection! Over such the second death has no power, but they shall be priests of God and of Christ, and they shall reign with him a thousand years.

For more than 1,500 years there have been two opposing interpretations of these words, one of which considers this to be a situation which in principle already existed in those days, or at least began shortly after. The other views this passage as a prophecy which will only take place in the last days. The reader of Revelation who is not aware of this difference will incline to the latter opinion and view the passage as a description of what will occur after chapter 19, which describes the victory of the returning Christ. However, since Augustine, and even earlier, there has been a theory which refused to read the visions of Revelation as a presentation of consecutive events but as a repetition of a constantly recurring motif. This is the so-called recapitulation theory. These interpreters point to chapter 12 which, in turn, points back to the birth of Christ and its successive salvation history described in new images differing from those of chapters 6 and 7. They find the same in chapter 20.

In chapter 19 Christ is already victor, and 20.7ff. describes the last struggle between Christ and his adversary. Thus, they conclude, in 20.1 John reaches back into history. The recapitulation theory stands on weak ground, however. Its only support is chapter 12 which points back to Christ's birth. For the rest, that which follows always builds upon the preceding. It clearly contains progress and climax which moves ahead in every detail. In 12.9 the devil is cast to earth, in 20.2 he is bound, in 20.10 he is cast into the lake of fire. According to 20.4 in the millennium the people are found who 'had not worshipped the beast or its image'. This obviously takes place after 13-19, which is also evident from verse 10—Gog and Magog are cast into the lake where the beast and the false prophet are already. For this reason we believe it unacceptable to say that chapter 20 points back into history. It evidently describes a phase which follows 13-17, but which immediately precedes the consummation. That there are recapitulating *elements* in Revelation is not excluded, but a *theory* of recapitulation does not present the key for insight into the book.

Within the passage itself interpretations separate, particularly at 20.4. They who read a present situation into the millennial reign point to the 'thrones' which elsewhere in Revelation are always in heaven, and to the 'souls' which remind one of 6.9, a word which signifies an incorporeal, other-worldly situation. This is not a strong argument. The word 'soul' is in biblical language not always an incorporeity. Moreover, the fact that the souls are seated upon thrones is described as 'the first resurrection' (20.6). That must then be interpreted as their incorporeal union with Christ in heaven, which would be a most unusual manner of speaking. It is more relevant to think here of a return to earth of the believers who have died. According to several interpreters I Cor. 15.42 and I Thess. 4.16f. point to this. It seems to me even more probable that the words 'they came to life' (Rev. 20.4) are an allusion to the Greek translation of Ezek. 37.10, and that they deal with Israel's recovery. For 20.7ff. agrees with Ezekiel 38 and 39, and

21 and 22 are full of allusions to Ezekiel 40-48. A closer examination of the manner in which Revelation cites the prophets (Ezekiel in particular) would shed more light on the subject. I dare draw no conclusions, and I can leave aside the questions which arise, since the decision does not fall here. Whether the souls are on earth or in heaven is of little consequence. The question is whether they will, according to verse 4, reign on *earth*. With those who view the kingdom of peace as being in the present the answer is negative. They see in verse 4 a description of the heavenly bliss of the martyrs which occurs outside the earth. But verses 5 and 6 clearly limit this blessed situation to one thousand years. Will their heavenly bliss disappear after the earthly period? This seems an odd idea. It is not clear to me how these exegetes deal with the connection between the souls' reign and the period of one thousand years. We cannot evade the thought that according to Revelation a period arrives in which Christ, after his victory over the antichrist, will reign over the earth with his saints, especially the martyrs (the word 'judgment' in verse 4 should be translated from the Hebrew idiom as 'reign'). The question whether only the martyrs reign, or whether they are a part of a large group of saints, we can leave unanswered. But there is certainly a connection with 6.9-11 where the souls of the martyrs cry out for vengeance, and where they are told to rest a little longer, because their number must first be completed. This evidently takes place after the period of the beast. The time for which the martyrs cried, the time which would prove that they died not for an illusion but for the living God, has in chapter 20 finally arrived.

That period lasts a thousand years. This, like all numbers in Revelation, is symbolic. It points to a particular duration, stability, and fulness. It is a contrast to the quick three-and-a-half-year fragment of life given to the beast. Yet, this period is not the consummation. Verses 7 to 10 picture a fierce reaction. There is evidently something superficial about this reign of Christ. The devil does not tempt man (vs. 3), that is, not to an open and massive revolt against the reign of Christ. But resistance boils under the surface. After the thousand years 'the nations from the four corners of the earth' are seduced by the devil so that they march against the focal point of earth, Jerusalem. The new order of life seemingly has had little influence in the dark corners of the earth removed from the cultural centre. That is the origin of the resistance under Gog and Magog. Ezekiel 38 and 39 are then being fulfilled. A situation precedes this as is described in Ezekiel 36 and 37—a temporary kingdom of peace with Israel as the centre.

Much remains unclear in Revelation 20. This is part of the obscurity of the whole book. But this minimal conclusion is justifiable: John expected that after the antichrist a long and happy period will arrive in which the boundaries between heaven and earth begin to disappear, the down-trodden will reign, the suffering Church of Christ will be publicly proved right, and the recovered Israel will be the centre of the world. A political and social order will rule in which the reign of Christ will be expressed as strong as is possible in a world from which sin, suffering, and death are not yet expelled.

The Background of this Confession

This vision is strangely isolated in the New Testament. There is a parallel in I Cor. 15.23-28, where Paul discusses the reign of Christ which begins with his return to earth, and which lasts until death has been overcome, Christ then returning the Kingdom to the Father. This is, indeed, another remarkable New Testament passage about history, which can be compared with II Thessalonians 2. From our distant vantage point we cannot clearly see its meaning. For Paul, as well as for John, Christ's victory seems to have several stages. It evolves. John and Paul in their own way express a common faith which evidently was a part of their faith in Christ. It is clear, however, that we cannot point out a definite connection with Revelation 20, and that Paul's words are too brief and enigmatic to throw any light on it. We must look elsewhere for help in finding the roots of the faith in a millennial kingdom.

The history of religion does not offer us this help. We do find there speculations about thousand-year periods, and Parsiism (Zarathustra's religion) knows about saviours, and redeemers, who appear in the last three periods, but such a periodization of world events is not present in Revelation. That is why Jewish thought which viewed history as a week in which a day represents a thousand years of which the last will be the 'world sabbath' does not help us very much either. At the most this can explain why John speaks of a thousand years. We find help only when we turn to the Jewish conception of the so-called 'Age of the Messiah' which lived in the apocalypses as well as the rabbis, especially in the age in which Revelation was written. They expected the arrival of a period (often called 'the age of the Messiah') before the consummation. During this period and under the direction of the Messiah a new order of life, which will represent the maximum of beneficence, peace, and prosperity possible in a world subject to sin and death, will be introduced. This period is briefly described in IV Ezra and limited to four hundred years (IV Ezra 7.26-29). The 'Syriac Baruch' (probably the end of first century AD) describes this period in detail, almost as the land of Cockaigne (see chapters 29, 40, 73, and 74). Much of what we read there reappears in early Christian writers. Enoch 93 discusses an eighth world-week of temporary well-being, and the Sibylline Oracles also present a vague indication of such an intermediate kingdom (VII, 652ff.). These are the apocalyptic writings. The rabbinic expressions are admittedly from later centuries, but they contain old traditions. Their opinion is not far removed from IV Ezra, but there is great difference about the duration of the Messianic Age. There is mention of 40, 70, 100, 400, 1,000, or 2,000 years.

These texts are not a direct help. Actually none of them is similar to Revelation 20. The core of the latter is the resurrection of the dead, at least of the martyrs, and the idea that a resurrection will take place during the millennial kingdom appears in the rabbis only at the beginning of the third century. All these more or less close parallels become meaningful only when we seek the roots of this Jewish doctrine concerning the Messianic Age which is to precede the Kingdom of God. The traditional answer to this question is that the Old Testament prophets assumed Kingdom of God to be an earthly situation with Israel as its centre. Later writers began more and more to see a contrast between this world and that of the future. In order still to be able to place the prophets' visions they supposed that there would be a Messianic Kingdom before the Kingdom of God. This reasoning is not acceptable, however. In the chapter about history in the Old Testament we already saw that one really cannot speak of a twofold faith; on the one hand the prophets' faith in an earthly kingdom, and on the other hand the other-worldly kingdom of others. Moreover, this would be of little help with Revelation since there the ancient prophetic figures, especially from Ezekiel, are not applied to the millennial kingdom, but only to the Kingdom of God. This way of thinking is quite intellectualistic. It seems as though the apocalyptists spent many painful hours in their study in order to find a way to harmonize the two traditions. If they saw two traditions, and *if* they wished to harmonize these, and *if* as a result of this they developed the concept of an intermediate kingdom, it must at least have had deeper roots than that of a religious or intellectual drive for combination.

These roots are not too difficult to discover. In this we must note the variations in duration ascribed to the Messianic Age. This is not arbitrary. Behind the different numbers is the common conviction that the period of 'refreshing' will correspond with and counterbalance the time of oppression which God's people experienced. The prayer from Ps. 90.15 played an important role in this. 'Make us glad as many days as thou hast afflicted us, and as many years as we have seen evil.' Some combine this with Gen. 15.13 where God tells Abraham that his people will live in oppression four hundred years (in Egypt). That is why the Messianic Age will last four hundred years. Similarly one could reckon forty years from the period of the wilderness journey and seventy from that of the exile. Ps. 90.15 also played its role in the case of other numbers. The number of days of blessing will balance the number of days of affliction. God will triumph not only in the future kingdom, but also in this dispensation he will assure us that besides the indications of his impotence there will also be indications of his sovereignty. These will appear just when the power of the evil one will seem to drown all God's creation.

The writer of Revelation possessed this same faith. The days of God's affliction remind him of the martyrs in Revelation 6, the days of the Church's persecution. They partook of the cross of Christ. They will also take part in his resurrection within the boundaries of this world which rejected him. In this way Revelation gives this Jewish conviction a new reality and a new form through the crucified and resurrected Christ.

We now notice that the underlying faith of Revelation 20 is the same as the faith of Paul which is the basis of Romans 9-11. In the latter it concerns God's faithfulness to Israel, in the former it concerns the martyrdom of the Christian Church and the blessing of the whole world. We shall not discuss the details. It is very difficult for a Westerner to understand all the imagery of Revelation, let alone to make it a part of himself. With these two passages in mind, along with I Cor. 15.23-28 and the other matters touched upon in this chapter, we may safely say that our being able to expect great things to happen during this dispensation for the sake of God's faithfulness and God's honour (these two are one), just when the need is greatest, is essential to the faith of the New Testament.

The Church and Chiliasm

But the Christian Church did not accept this faith as her own, and she certainly did not find strength and joy in it.

On the contrary, the doctrine of the millennium has through the centuries been a bone of contention. We cannot neglect to examine this unfortunate situation a little more closely.

In the early Christian Church, faith in a millennium was universal. We find it in Papias, in the Epistle of Barnabas, in Justin Martyr, Irenaeus, Tertullian, Hippolytus, and Lactantius. Justin (*c.* 150) discusses it in *Dialogue with Trypho*. The Kingdom of the Messiah will arise in Palestine (139.4), Jerusalem will be rebuilt, and there will be a time of well-being and joy for Jewish and Gentile Christians (80.1). Justin discusses it in sober expressions. He believes that the millennium is closely connected with the restoration of Israel. He also states that many pious Christians do not share this conviction (80.2), an observation which probably does not mean faith in a kingdom of peace in general, but in Israel's restoration. The descriptions of the millennium by many of the early Church's writers barely sound like Revelation 20 with its soberness and Christocentrism; they rather sound like the paradise of the Syriac Apocalypse of Baruch. This kind of realism roused the disgust of Greek spiritualism, which influenced Christian intellectuals. The master of synthesis between Hellenism and Christian faith, the Alexandrian Origen (*c.* 200), rejected Revelation as not being a part of the New Testament canon. In the Western part of the early Church the expectation of a millennium was in one way or another frustrated by the church Father, Augustine, who at first shared this faith on the basis of the above speculations concerning world-week and world-sabbath, but who was later convinced of the correctness of the recapitulation theory. For centuries his opinion that Revelation 20 describes the reign of the Church from Christ's advent cast the die against the expectation of a millennial kingdom, not only for the Middle Ages and the Roman Catholic Church, but also for the Reformation which, moreover, was even more discouraged by the Anabaptists' excesses. The Lutheran Augsburg Confession judges this doctrine as 'Jewish opinions', and the Reformed Second

Helvetic Confession calls it 'Jewish dreams'. The repeated reproach of the Reformation churches is that the so-called chiliasts (*chilias* means 'thousand'), like the Jews, cherish for the future an earthly and physical expectation, and pay no attention to the heavenly and spiritual nature of God's Kingdom as taught in the New Testament. Yet, chiliasm maintained itself through the centuries not only outside or on the periphery of the Church (where it has taken an important place, from the Bogomiles and Catharists to modern Adventist groups), but also within the Church. The well-known Würtemberg pietist, Bengel, was a convinced chiliast, and there have been an impressive number of theologians during the nineteenth and twentieth centuries who in one way or another expected a future kingdom of peace. We must, however, differentiate between the forms of this expectation within the Church proper, and those of the sects or fundamentalists, although the boundaries cannot be drawn too sharply. We shall begin with the latter, which have innumerable supporters throughout the world, and possess, particularly in Britain and the United States, a sea of literature practically unknown in the Church. Although there are many differences, there is general agreement that one day, probably soon, the real believers will suddenly disappear from the earth because they will be taken into heaven to be with Christ. The believers who have died will then be resurrected. The unconverted Jews return to Palestine where some of them will accept the faith. The antichrist will come from Israel, and will persecute those who have been converted. This is the seventieth week of Dan. 9.27, 'the time of Jacob's oppression', which is also described in Matthew 24. The millennial kingdom will come after the antichrist's defeat. Christ descends to the earth with his saints in order to reign; according to Ezekiel 40-48 the temple is restored, Jerusalem is rebuilt, and services of sacrifice are resumed not as a shadow of what is to come, but as an indication of the coming fulfilment.

The tenacity and extent of chiliasm are a reaction to the spiritualism and the lack of historical perspective of the official Church which saw no future for the world, spiritualized the prophecies, and limited her expectation to personal salvation in heaven. He who realizes this will have little desire to attack the chiliasts' opinions, let alone ridicule them. He will understand that they will not disappear until their truth has been accepted into the confession and life of the whole Church. Until that day arrives, chiliasm will continue to captivate many, especially among the simple folk, with its faithfulness to the Scriptures ánd the concreteness of its expectation for the world.

On the other hand, it must also be said that chiliasm offers us little help for a re-examination of these matters. This is first due to its view of Scripture. The Bible is for these so-called Fundamentalists purely a divine book which contains many exact, although very dispersed, communications concerning future events. They have no appreciation for the human character of biblical writings and for the opinions and environment of the times in which they were written. All biblical books fall under the same category, namely, that of divine information. That is how they can see in the seventy weeks of Daniel 9 a detailed prophecy of Israel's future. More information about this seventieth week of years can be found in Matthew 24 and Revelation. But there are many centuries between the sixty-ninth week of years (of Christ's appearance) and the seventieth week of years (of Israel's future). That is the day of the Church, who has no earthly promises such as Israel but who at the end of her day (an intermediate time in God's plan of salvation) will be taken into heaven. Daniel knew nothing about that day of the Church. The first information about it is found in Paul's words concerning the secret revealed to him (Eph.; Col.). The Scripture is a puzzle and the pieces must be sought everywhere.

The prophecies are considered to be literal. In this respect liberalism and fundamentalism draw their strength from the same root in Western thought. Neither has appreciation for the poetic, nor for the fact that realities which are far removed from experience—including the experience of faith—can be understood only through figurative language: a language which we can only partly translate into the Western language of facts and ideas.

We have already seen that chiliasm makes a sharp distinction between different 'dispensations'. A ruling factor is the contrast between the dispensation of Israel with its earthly promises, and the dispensation of the Church with her heavenly promises. The New Testament indeed makes a distinction between Israel and the dispensation of the Church, but only in the sense of two recipients of salvation, and not of a twofold salvation. Since the chiliasts construe the latter, their thought is not true to the biblical historicity. According to them, history, in the sense we have used the word here, ended in Acts 28 when Paul separated himself from the earthly Israel, and devoted himself entirely to the increase of the Church; and it will begin again only after the Church will have been taken from the earth. Our time is an intermediate time during which it is a matter simply of the salvation of the individual in heaven, just as (and even worse than) is the case in the faith of the Church in general. Worse, because they ascribe all the words concerning a visible church and organization to Israel, and they see little value in the modern missionary endeavour, since a fruitful proclamation will take place only during the millennial kingdom, by a converted Israel.

Thus, chiliasm exists because of artificial combinations and divisions. It works entirely and solely with biblical materials. The essence of chiliasm is the manner in which this material is arranged with chronological precision. In almost all chiliastic books one can find tables, surveys, and drawings to make the chiliastic chronology easier to understand. It is precisely this chronology which cannot be found in the Bible. Daniel does not say that there is a long period of time between the penultimate and the last week of years. Paul does not say that he is discussing this intermediate time in Ephesians and Colossians. Revelation does not state that it is limited to that last week of years. Ezekiel knows nothing of long periods of time between the events which he foresees.

Jesus himself nowhere reveals the knowledge that he is aware of a very near dispensation of the Church. We could continue in this vein. The framework of chiliasm—and that is its essence—has no biblical foundation, and is purely a human or rather a Western mould in which the biblical facts are placed or pressed: a mould which owes its existence and its continuance to a certain intellectualist drive to localize everything.

Chiliasm wishes to know more than we are able to know. Many books of the Bible discuss history and the consummation. The way in which each did this is according to the light received from God, and always in the idiom of the opinions of his own time. All of these witnesses endeavour to present *one* reality, but there is a great difference in imagery and in depth and breadth. We are dealing with a plurality of projections of what will eventually be *one* vision and *one* expectation. The same is in fact true of all the religious concepts of the Bible, even the Christological ideas of the various New Testament writers. The Church needed centuries of thoughtful study before it understood the normative unity. Such a study has hardly begun in connection with the concepts of history and the consummation. The time for this has now arrived. We cannot reproach the chiliasts for thinking wrongly about these things and at the same time continue to neglect real thought in the matter.

If we now return to the doctrine of the millennium in particular, our objection to the chiliasts is that they give a central place to this doctrine which it does not have in the Holy Scriptures. The chiliasts will disagree at this point, since they ascribe all eschatological concepts of the Old Testament prophecies to this Jewish kingdom of peace. Strangely enough, the Revelation of John itself does not do this. The kingdom of the consummation which comes *after* the kingdom of peace and *after* the battle with Gog and Magog—*that* is described by the presentations of the Old Testament prophets (Rev. 21, 22), and *not* the millennial kingdom. This is discussed only (probably) in connection with Ezekiel 36 and 37. This is a difficult fact for the chiliasts.

They naturally point to the fact that in the prophetic visions of the future, Israel and Palestine are central, and that this is difficult to ascribe to the fulfilment of the end. But this did not prevent the writer of Revelation from ascribing them to it. This proves that the prophecies had for him a strong element of figurative speech, or at least that he did not consider the Old Testament to be a puzzle, or that he saw fluid boundaries between the kingdom of peace and the eternal Kingdom, just as we can see fluid boundaries between the dispensations of the past and future Israel and that of the Church. In these different dispensations it is evidently a matter of one and the same salvation. Some supporters of chiliasm try to justify it with the idea of 'pre-fulfilment'. But this only makes the chiliastic scheme more complicated. The facts it desires to explain demand that it breaks with the scheme itself.

I have already mentioned that along with the fundamentalistic concept of the kingdom of peace, there exists one within the official Church, although the boundary cannot be clearly distinguished. This 'chiliasm of the Church' is more widespread than is usually believed. The emphasis among church supporters of this concept is not as strong as among Fundamentalists. But a long series of theologians has expressed its faith in a still future maximum development of the power of Christ and the Spirit within this dispensation. We may begin by mentioning Eusebius of Caesarea who saw the arrival of the kingdom of peace in the appearance of Constantine the Great, and for that reason stands between the opinions of the official Church and chiliasts. We omit the Middle Ages which saw the chiliasts particularly in antichurch movements. Since the Reformation we find such names as Piscator, Alsted, Cocceius, Jurieu, W. à Brakel, Vitringa, Comenius, Bengel, von Oetinger, Auberlen, da Costa, Chantepie de la Saussaye, Sr, Gunning, Van Oosterzee, Kuyper; and among the theologians of today Cullmann, Haitjema, Miskotte, K. L. Schmidt, and Vogel. I found chiliastic leanings even in the Eastern Orthodox theologian Sergius Bulgakov.[4] Moreover, if we include the verbal pronouncements of many important theologians, we must admit that at least the modern Reformation churches are not antichiliastic. This can be said with reference to many theologians, and probably too in the light of what is taking place in the life of the Church. But there is a general fear of studying these matters too closely and of placing them in a broader context. But to avoid doing so prevents their enriching the life of the Church.

The Meaning of the Kingdom of Peace

Before we leave this subject we return to the significance of this confession concerning a future kingdom of peace. Many theologians have made important observations about this. Kuyper views the millennial kingdom as 'a last call to the conscience'. De Roos says, 'The millennial kingdom is God's great offer to the world, the great opportunity for conversion.'[5] Yet, these definitions are still too narrow, because they are too legalistic. Besides, the offer of repentance in Revelation 20 and related passages, although it is assumed, is not in the foreground. Miskotte finds the reality of the kingdom of peace in the conviction that 'history must find its completion in history itself'.[6] K. L. Schmidt expresses it this way: 'The millennial kingdom represents the triumph of Christ and his Church in the heart of the world and, also over the world.'[7] In the kingdom of peace Bulgakov sees the curve of history bend so far upwards that it meets heaven; the boundary between heaven and earth, which will later disappear completely, already begins to recede. Cullmann says approximately the same: 'In this kingdom the end of our time already reaches into the new creation.' This is also Bietenhard's opinion. Quistorp's formulation is felicitous, and discusses the Kingdom of God 'which although it ends history, with its coming nevertheless erects a last sign of the consummation of history, since *this* world will be transformed in the new world of God'.[8] Kantonen is of the opinion that, 'It expresses the connection between history and the new world, is testimony of judgment on the present world, and guards the realism of the Christian hope against mystical world-denial.' He explains this by pointing to the meaning of this confession in our time for social justice.[9] Schrenk speaks of 'a prophetic push forward in the time of the transition of the ages'.[10] The explanation of Van Oosterzee is most striking.[11] He views the millennium as a parallel with the forty days between the resurrection and the ascension. Just as the power of Christ's resurrection received a certain historical expansion in this old world, so later this will also be the case with the Church. 'Golgotha is already [during the millennium] behind his Church, and without having ascended it, her Mount of Olives is in sight.'

As an addition to this I would define the meaning of the doctrine of the kingdom of peace in the following manner: Christ was crucified in this world, but he was also raised from the dead. The history which begins with his coming and which is inaugurated by the missionary proclamation is an analogy of this reality. In the form of the antichrist the power of evil once more receives the opportunity to turn against Christ throughout the full breadth of the cosmic front. God's honour and might demand that he give his adversaries the opportunity to reveal their power. But his honour and might also demand that the resurrection of Christ in history be revealed throughout the full breadth of the cosmic front, as far as this is possible in this dispensation: in the restoration of Israel and in many other signs. This will be the spiritual analogue in this world to the forty days. Since sin and death still reign, a brief but fierce setback is unavoidable. But this represents the transition to the union of heaven and earth, which is reflected in the kingdom of peace by the abolition of their boundaries. The labour pains of the Kingdom began with the coming of Christ. In spite of and during suffering it continues. The triumph over the antichrist makes it clear that redemption is nigh, although there is one more contraction to suffer. Our history is God's and Christ's, as history itself will make plain.

The Development of God's Kingdom in History

We shall encounter an earthly analogy not only of the cross, but also of the resurrection. This presses us to ask again about the present in view of this insight into the future. We return, therefore, to the matters which occupied our attention at the beginning of this chapter.

Abraham Kuenen, the distinguished progenitor of modern theology, in 1875 published a booklet about the millennial kingdom which contains some instructive passages even for the present. Although he rejected the myth of a coming kingdom of peace, he finds in this myth a beneficial dissatisfaction with what is, and a firm faith in a better future here on earth. In that sense he chooses for chiliasm against a satisfied and complacent Church. God does not leave the work of his hands undone, but he continues it. Since, however, an improvement from without cannot be of long duration, his conclusion is, 'Our chiliasm can be no other than a fervent and active faith in moral and social progress.'[12] Kuenen chooses against the expressed opinion that the Kingdom of God will fall into our midst like a bomb at the end of time, and he chooses for the faith that the Kingdom of God grows through the labour of human hands. These two concepts have long been two alternatives. This was clearly evident in Stockholm at the Conference for Life and Work (1925). The Germans in particular represented the first opinion, and the Americans the latter. It is remarkable to note that traditional orthodoxy, which maintained the first opinion, yet loved expressions like 'co-operating in the expansion of God's Kingdom'. This raises the suspicion that we are not dealing with a real alternative. The Kingdom of God is the work of God himself. This is the truth in the orthodox position. The error is to believe that it must therefore be a sudden event entirely from without. God is active in the world. The Kingdom of God grows. This is the truth in the liberal position. The error is to believe that it is therefore man's labour, and that it is identical with moral and social progress. After two world wars there will be few who can completely accept Kuenen's words. It is time, however, to give a rightful place in the whole of Christian faith to the position held by Kuenen. In saying this we do not forget that along with the growth of the Kingdom of God the antichristian powers will also grow. This fact is often used as an argument against the idea of growth for the Kingdom of God. But the negative growth is in our broken world the negative side and shadow of the positive growth. It is also an indication of the fact that Christ has assumed dominion.

In this chapter, however, we are concerned with the positive growth. We believe in a God who continues his work victoriously in this dispensation. This is a faith. It is based on the fact that Christ was raised from the dead in this old world. It is not disturbed by the fact that experience often seems to contradict this faith. It knows that to God the facts are in agreement with this faith. When he looks back into history, looks around in the present, reads his newspaper, and listens to what is happening, the believer expects that he will *see* God's goodness in the land of the living (Ps. 27.13). In that sense, too, there is a 'waiting on the Lord'. And there *is* vision, even in our present. We see how the missionary endeavour has planted the young churches everywhere, just before the doors of the East are closed to the West. In a time when the world is driven to closer unity, we see that this is with increasing tempo the case with Christ's Church, so that the unified world will later find in her a prophetic and priestly counterpart (*Gegenüber*). We see how Israel, in spite of the most radical attempts to wipe it from the earth, has survived and is returning to the land of promise, and is undergoing a complete rejuvenation and renewal. We see that Christ's order of life forcefully progresses throughout the world—through aid to the underdeveloped nations—against the old naturalistic patterns of life. And certainly we can see under, beside, and against all this, the growth of the opposition forces. The first should not blind us to the second. This was discussed earlier. Here we must say with emphasis that the second should not blind us to the first either. This is even more true since the second would not exist without the presence of the first. The growth of the opposition forces, then, is an indication of the growth of the Kingdom of God.

God's Kingdom and Progress

The above indications are derived not only from the life of the Church, but also from the life of the world. For in so far as there was a concept of history in the Christian Church, it was usually an uncritical and one-sided orientation to the Church itself. Uncritical because people identified God's work with the work of the Church and ignored the fact that the Christian Church is the place where the antichrist makes his nest. One-sided because they did not see that Christ's dominion is broader than the Church, and that it is revealed wherever his order of life asserts itself against naturalism's lack of freedom and anarchism's chaos in order to bring man nearer to his human destiny. A great number of men are in the service of Christ's dominion without knowing or wanting to be: intellectuals, artists, physicians, nurses, educators, social workers, technicians, and those taking part in technical assistance to underdeveloped nations, but also, and no less, the mothers who pass Christ's order of life on to their children. These and many others are in the service of Christ—who has compassion for the creation which waits with eager longing for its deliverance (Rom. 8.19-22). He wishes to gain more ground for the new order of life which he came to bring as a small beginning of what he later will be able to present in perfection. What we call progress in the world also originates in him. This concept came into the world only after and through Christianity. This progress is often of an antichristian nature, but this, too, is an indication that it originates in him. And more often it is not of this nature; it is then a simple objective service which opens man's way to a more perfect humanity, or even leads him to the road where he can encounter Christ.

While the coming return of Christ 'absorbs' the world, it creates in man this untiring longing 'for a better world'; and we recognize progress as the result of this longing. . . . Progress is at all times a hidden fruit of the Easter victory, by which sinful man remains in spite of all king and creation.[13]

Novelists and poets are often more aware of the connection between Christ's dominion and everyday life than the theologians. Thus Achterberg describes the cleaning-woman, and then continues:

> God will one day find her on his ground,
> Walking the golden streets towards his throne,
> Clanging the dustpan with her broom.
> Symbols will be changed to cymbals in the
> Hour of death. . . .[14]

Nijhoff describes a room in which a party had just stopped, and everything is now dirty and wilted. But above this is the promise: I make all things new. As an indication of this the cleaning-woman arrives in the morning:

> Ah, see how fresh the house becomes!
> Without she shines the copper name-plate.
> How shiny it becomes, how spotless!
> The desert shall blossom as a rose.[15]

In his poem about the surgeon Guillaume van der Graft is still more aware of this connection:

> . . . He has a prophetic hand
> Like the one of which God said, 'Write;
> I hate death like a tumour
> And suffering like a carcinoma.
> Obey and write: I restore
> Life again unto my fondest dream!'
> We do not know what he believes,
> It makes no difference to me;
> Whenever he anaesthetizes man,
> He does it for the sake of Christ. . . .[16]

Certainly only one step is necessary to turn all that has been said here into a lie; namely, when we forget that all the forces released by Christ can work not only for him, but also against him. The surgeon can work to build a brave new world which knows no higher ideals than those of undisturbed hygienic and economic well-being. This is not implied in his work itself, however, nor in the fact that he may be an unbeliever. He is fighting for a matter for which we learned to fight as a consequence of the way in which God historized the world. These forces he can, of course, use against Christ, as, for instance, happened in Nazi medicine in the concentration camps. His work is then judged. Also, without his desire or knowledge, its objective could be serviceable to secularism and nihilism. In that case as a human being he is co-responsible and must question the framework in which he works. Nevertheless his work as such will remain good, and a prophecy of Christ's kingdom of peace. In the struggle for a genuine human existence, for deliverance of the suffering, for the elevation of the underdeveloped, for redemption of the captives, for the settlement of race and class differences, for opposition to chaos, crime, suffering, sickness, and ignorance—in short, in the struggle for what we call progress—an activity is taking place throughout the world to the honour of Christ. It is sometimes performed by people who know and desire it; it is more often performed by those who have no concern for it, but whose labour proves that Christ truly received—in full objectivity—all power on earth.

The Visibility of Christ's Conquest

During the centuries of progress, since 1700, the Christian Church has not recognized this. This is understandable for the reasons enumerated in chapter 5, 'The Missionary Endeavour as a History-Making Force'. Progress was usually carried on by men who were strangers to the Church of Christ, and even by those who used progress as a weapon against him and his Church. This led to a Christian pessimism of culture which brings its own judgment with it because it blinds men to all the aspects of the Lord's salvation discussed in this chapter. The average Christian does not expect to see any positive signs of Christ's reign in the world. He believes that the world only becomes worse and races in the direction of the antichrist. He has a feeling that God looks on, powerless, and that God will have his chance in the far future through a sudden interference. The average Christian is not aware of the presence of the Kingdom in the world today. But he is prepared to believe in the presence of Christ in his personal life, in prosperity as well as adversity. It is sometimes very moving to see how strong this faith can be, even and particularly in the darkest hours. But it is depressing to see how helpless and fearful this same Christian often is when he reads his newspaper or when he thinks about his children's future. Prevalent in our churches is a bad kind of pietism (there are other kinds) which limits the power of Christ to his personal relationship to the individual believer, and which sees no connection between Christ and world-events, or between Christ and daily work. This leads to an ungrateful blindness for the signs of Christ's reign in the present. Expressions such as 'we live on the edge of a volcano', 'it can't last this way much longer', 'humanity is steadily becoming worse', 'the end of time is near' are very popular in Christian circles. And they believe that this pessimism of culture (if this attitude at all deserves such a serious name) is completely in agreement with Christian faith. It is indeed true that these complaints are not baseless even in what God reveals about the world. But it is at most a half-truth. There should be reason for great wonderment, just because everything looks so threatening. The fact that we can still *live* on the edge of the volcano, in the midst of secularism and nihilism, is a tremendous miracle which can be understood and observed only in the light of Christ's already-active conquest. We should not be surprised that a Christless or even antichristian autonomy and ideology threatens to disintegrate life. On the contrary, these forces are repeatedly limited, held back, turned back, or converted by the positive signs of Christ's reign in the world, and this tremendous fact should fill us constantly with gratitude and amazement, giving us power to enter the future without fear and with the expectation of seeing new signs.

In modern times this was particularly seen and expressed by the elder Blumhardt, who cannot be said to have been unaware of the antichristian forces in the world. But he knew fully that Christ is the victor. His anger was therefore often roused against the Christian pessimism for the future. He believed that a 'time of grace' was near at hand, and that the coming great tribulation, which preoccupied his fellow Christians, would seem much shorter than it was usually supposed.[17]

The Relationship between Cross and Resurrection in History

We cannot close this chapter without making reference to the connection between what has been discussed here and the content of the preceding chapter. At the beginning of this chapter we mentioned that cross and resurrection are not active in the same history-making capacity. This is connected with their different function in the history of salvation. The cross stands firmly and concretely in the centre of our history. The resurrection stands vaguely at its periphery. It, too, receives expansion: Christologically in the forty days, pneumatologically in sanctification, and historically in the manner discussed above. But in the present dispensation there is no balance between cross and resurrection, let alone an ascendancy of the resurrection. The last and greatest result of the cross is the reign of the antichrist, but the ultimate result of the resurrection is connected with the new heaven and the new earth. It is beyond the boundaries of this dispensation. This is inherent in its essence. The resurrection life destroys sin and death, and by doing so ends the old dispensation. The indications of Christ's reign in the present, the return of Israel, and the kingdom of peace introduced by these, are no more than small signs in comparison with the glory that will be revealed to us. Even the greatest indication which takes place in this dispensation could be belittled and explained differently, as is now the case with many believers who do not see the signs they witness. The signs will be great for him who understands by faith, and it will bring those without faith to amazement and reflection. But the question is whether it will be more than this. All ambiguity will disappear only at the consummation. Then every eye shall see him.

Here our road meets that of the modern Roman Catholic philosophy of history, and it would be well to take note. Especially since the Second World War there has been a high interest in the questions discussed in this book among the Germans and French. A large volume of literature has been written on this subject. Protestant theology cannot compare with it, and this material is little known among us. There are two distinct lines of thought in this literature. The first places the emphasis on the fact that the Kingdom is supernal, that it is solely God's work, and that it comes through the destruction of this sinful world. Evil cannot be exterminated from this world. The gospel, embodied in the Church, calls to life a conflict which increases in violence till the end, when it destroys the shape of the world. The forces of the Kingdom of God are already active in the world, but they cannot be indicated. In the end our attitude can be no other than one of waiting and hope. These words approximately characterize the bases of the philosophy of history of men like Congar and Daniélou.

Opposed to these is a group of thinkers who were greatly influenced by the famous Jesuit biologist and theologian, Teilhard de Chardin, and his evolutionary ideas on nature and history. Montuclard, Dubarle, and Thils are representatives of this school. To them, the incarnation means the beginning of a new development of mankind. They place the emphasis on the Christian 'leaven' in culture. Grace penetrates human nature and prepares it in a mysterious but effective way for the heavenly Jerusalem. In other words, it develops a mankind grounded in love as the highest phase of evolution in nature and history.

If translated into our categories, we might say that the first group considers history as the stage where Christ is crucified, and the second views it as the scene of his resurrection power. If on the side of the Reformation an equally intense study of the theology of history were to be made, perhaps people would there choose the first-named opinion. These scholars are indeed closer to us. The evolutionary incarnationalism of the second group appears unbiblical to us. We cannot readily accept the role they ascribe to man and his co-operation. Yet, the tension between these two groups of Christian scholars is an indication that every one-sidedness in the Christian theology of history misses the truth. Roman Catholic theologians, too, realize that both lines of thought must be connected (Malevez, Hugo Rahner, and lately Daniélou). The question is, however, how. The scholars mentioned above offer little help in answering this question. They primarily study the problems philosophically, rather than through biblical theology. Moreover, both groups see the actual meaning of history as 'the struggle of the Church against the power of evil'.[18] In view of the fact that in the thinking of these writers the Church is identical with the Roman Catholic Church, we consider this viewpoint to be too narrow, as we argued earlier. Our greatest objection is to the duality of natural and supernatural existence, in which history can never be more than an instrument and a vehicle to bring the Church to her destiny. Christ, however, is not concerned about the Church as such, but that in and through the Church he might be glorified in the hearts of men and within the sphere of history.

If we try ourselves to answer the question of the connection between the two opinions, then the answer must move in different directions. In the first place, cross and resurrection are both together the secret of history. Lack of appreciation for either of the two factors or the isolation of one from the other as, for instance, is done when the power of the resurrection is considered active only in the Church, must be rejected. Secondly, there is no equilibrium between cross and resurrection. The shadows created by Christ's reign are completely a part of this dispensation, while the light of his reign will remain dim to the end. In the third place, we come closest to the secret of history when we see it as a parallel of what Christ does in the life of an individual and of the Church. The believer is and remains a sinner who finds life in justification by grace alone. At the same time he finds a real but contested and often interrupted sanctification of his life. This sanctification calls us away from the peace of paganism, but it does not yet grant us the peace of the saints. Our life is marked by struggle. For sanctification calls the opposition of the flesh to life, but is never completely overcome by the flesh. Conversely, neither does the Spirit overcome the flesh, and the surest indication of his activity is often the confession of guilt and repentance. Sanctification is 'a small beginning of obedience' (Heidelberg Catechism, answer 114).

But we must not stretch this parallel too far; man is something other than history. But it has much to say when we seek the manner in which the Spirit is present in a sinful world. He is represented in the form of struggle and the small beginning. Antinomianism and perfectionism are excluded in the discussion of history, as in that of sanctification. In spite of everything that can be said about the cross, the last word here too is: 'In all these things we are more than conquerors through him who loved us' (Rom. 8.37).

NOTES

[1] G. Schrenk in *TWNT* (IV, p. 218).

[2] *Church Dogmatics* II/2.

[3] For the sake of God's faithfulness must not we, in accordance with the prophets, expect the return of the so-called ten lost tribes? No. After the Babylonian captivity there is no longer any allusion to this because not two but twelve tribes returned. See I Chron. 9.1, 3; Ezra 6.17; 8.35; Acts 26.7; James 1.1. Moreover, during that period several tribes are mentioned by name.

[4] In *Du Verbe Incarné*, Paris, 1943, p. 376.

[5] De Roos, *Ned. Theol. Tijdschrift* VI, 1952, p. 228.

[6] Miskotte, *Hoofsdsom der Historie*, Nijkerk, 1945, p. 415.

[7] Schmidt, cited by Bietenhard, *Das Tausendjährige Reich*, Zürich, 1955, p. 63.

[8] H. Quistorp, *Die Letzten Dinge im Zeugnis Calvins*, Gütersloh, 1941, p. 165.

[9] T. A. Kantonen, *The Christian Hope*, Philadelphia, 1954, p. 69.

[10] G. Schrenk, *Die Weissagung über Israel im N.T.*, Zürich, 1951, p. 54.

[11] J. J. van Oosterzee, *Christelijke Dogmatiek*, Utrecht, 1872, vol. II/2, pp. 899-902.

[12] A. Kuenen, *Het Duizenjarig Rijk*, Amsterdam, 1875, vol. II/1, p. 77; also pp. 69-74.

[13] These quotations were taken from the article by Georges Casalis, 'Eschatologie und Fortschrift', *Unterwegs* V, 1951, pp. 261-72. Both quotations are found on p. 266.

[14] G. Achterberg, *Hoonte*, 1949, p. 29.

[15] M. Nijhoff, 'Voor Dag en Dauw', sixth sonnet in *Verzameld Werk*, 1954, vol. I, p. 448.

[16] Guillaume van der Graft, *Landarbeid*, 1951, p. 34.

[17] See the well-known biography by Friedrich Zündel, *Johann Christoph Blumhardt*, Giessen, 1926, espec. pp. 229-40.

[18] L. Malevez, *Deux Théologies Catholiques de l'Histoire* in *Bydragen* (of the Dutch Jesuits) X, 1949, p. 226.

8

THE CONSUMMATION OF HISTORY

> Whatever is true, whatever is honourable, whatever is just, whatever is pure, whatever is lovely, whatever is gracious, in the whole creation, in heaven and earth, is brought together in the future City of God. But it is renewed, recreated, and developed to its greatest glory. The material for it is present in this creation.
>
> H. Bavinck, *Gereformeerde Dogmatiek*, Kampen, 1911, vol. IV, p. 802.

Break and Connection

TALK ABOUT history is talk about consummation. Cross and resurrection are not in balance with each other. The resurrection has the ascendancy and victory over the cross. The cross will come to full revelation in this world, but this revelation will be relieved so that the world will have a full share in the resurrection of Christ. Resurrection is the essence of the consummation.

Therefore, to talk about consummation is to talk about a *break*. This world will be raised from its brokenness due to guilt and suffering, and will leave the *Gestalt* of the cross behind. This means that it will become a completely new world. But it is also true that whoever talks about consummation also talks about *connection*. It is the same world which will rise from its broken position. Our expectation of the future includes both break and connection, discontinuity and continuity. If the crucified and resurrected Christ is revealed in history, then the consummation will mean a radical break with all the forces which hinder his dominion. At the same time the consummation will be the continuation of the resurrection forces which already are active in history.

We must be careful with the use of the word 'continuation', however. It is completely different from 'to continue in the same vein'. The greatest unfolding of the forces of the resurrection in our history is only a small beginning. They are no more than harbingers of the future for which God has destined the world. They are crocuses in the winter of a fallen world. Moreover, they are so intertwined with the forces of evil that it is difficult for us to imagine what the world will be like when these forces are set free and reach their full potential. A special intervention from above is necessary to accomplish this. It will be the return of the resurrected Lord himself. Connection can be maintained and progress will become possible only by means of such a break with what is. But we must add with emphasis that it is a matter of the former—the connection and not the break. It is a matter of the break only because it serves the connection.

The favourite Jewish figure of speech regarding the 'labour pains of the Messiah' is apposite. They form the transition between this world and that of the future. The pains are a part of this world. They seem to stand in sharp contrast with the new world. Yet, they do not prove the absence of the future world, but precisely its hidden presence. The new world does not fall into the old like a bomb, nor does it take the place of the old which is destroyed, but it is born through the old in which it had been active. Although it is active, it is hidden to the extent that it can come into existence only through an unshackling, a redemption, and a great intervention. The external form of this world (*schema* in Greek) will pass away (I Cor. 7.31). We expect a new earth in the sense of a renewed one; this earth, but completely renewed. This world moves towards its end, but only because there it will meet its goal (the Greek word *telos* means 'end' as well as 'goal'). It is a goal, however, that can be reached only through an end, or a break.

History and consummation, then, are closely connected. The forces of the Kingdom, which are already active in history, will be loosed from the grip of sin and death in the consummation. In this respect the consummation is the crowning moment of history. But this crowning moment is at the same time the glorification by which history is placed above the possibilities known to us.

This is a parallel of what takes place in the personal life of the believer, particularly his physical existence. 'It is sown a physical body, it is raised a spiritual body' (I Cor. 15.44). These two bodies are not separated from each other. There is an essential connection, such as between the kernel and the ear (I Cor. 15.36ff.). But this connection is brought about by a break, even as Christ 'will change our lowly body to be like his glorious body' (Phil. 3.21). This change will be so tremendous that we must confess, 'it does not yet appear what we shall be, but we know that when he appears he shall be like him . . .' (I John 3.2). The resurrected Christ himself is the connection between my old and my new existence, and between our history and its consummation.

One may have noticed that in the traditional thinking of the Church greater emphasis is placed on the break than on the connection. In spite of the repeated expression 'the expansion of the Kingdom of God', which seems to point directly to a connection between this world and the next, the thought of a definite break, of a future which is strange and unrelated and which will fall into this evil world like a bomb, is far more alive. The other side of this is that this world is considered to be cancelled out, kept in order to be destroyed later. The above has made clear how one-sided, and therefore wrong and dangerous, this way of thinking is. This becomes even more evident when we discover how vigorously the connection between history and consummation is presented in the New Testament. In spite of all that is said there about the break, there is an almost unnoticeable transition from history into the consummation. This is true of every passage which deals with this situation: Matt. 24; Mark 13; Luke 21; I Cor. 15.23-30; II Thess. 2; and Rev. 18-22. It is sometimes difficult (especially in I Cor. 15) to say where the boundaries are because the consummation is simply presented as the continuation of history. It seems once again that the dualistic contrast between this world and the next which some believe discernible in inter-testamental Judaism and the New Testament as a contrast to the connection between both worlds in the proclamation of the prophets, is a construction which does not do justice to the truth. It is true that much is said about the future crisis in history and nature, but this does not take away the fact that the consummation is presented as taking place in the same time and space as history. Of course, we are dealing with figurative language. But figurative language is language which tries to say something, not nothing. And it tries to say that *this* world will be glorified, and that *this* history will be completed.

If we try to find the basis of the opinion that there is merely a break between history and consummation, we actually find only the well-known words of II Peter 3.5-13, where it is argued that since the first world was destroyed by water, the elements of the present world will melt away in fire in order to make room for a new earth. Here the break is indeed in the foreground. But after a more careful reading it seems that the connection is assumed, even as there was an essential connection between the world before and after the flood. The fire is an allusion to Isa. 66.15f. and other Old Testament passages. It is an indication of divine judgment which is active in testing and refining. It appears this way in other New Testament passages also (Mark 9.49; I Cor. 3.15; I Peter 1.7; Rev. 3.18). No matter how consuming its intervention may be, it refines; it does not destroy. Moreover, central to this are the words in verse 10 which according to the better manuscripts read: 'and the earth and the works that are therein will be found ["discovered" RV marg.; "laid bare" NEB]'. From earliest days this has seemed so strange to readers that 'found' was changed to 'burned up', or the negative 'not' was added, or in one way or another an attempt was made to change this reminder of a connection into an affirmation of the break. The whole passage is directed to those who dream about an eternal, undisturbed connection, and deny a coming break. Although this passage and others discuss the destruction of the world (Matt. 5.18; 24.35; I John 2.17), it is clear that we await not a destruction of the essence, but a change of the form (Matt. 5.5; I Cor. 7.31). This world and the next can never stand in absolute contrast, for the forces of the coming Age, Christ who is the firstfruit, and the Spirit who is the guarantee of our glorification, are already active in this world.

Time and Eternity

A proper view of the relationship between break and connection tends to be made more difficult by the ideas we, consciously or unconsciously, entertain about the relationship between *time*, which is a part of our world, and *eternity*, which we ascribe to the future world. Eternity is often identified with timelessness, and with deliverance from time. And because we cannot imagine anything outside of time, the consummation is entirely identified with the unthinkable and unimaginable. History and consummation are then mutually exclusive. This is very near to saying that time belongs to a guilty and fallen world, so that time, transience, and sin are always thought of together. This opinion is very popular in modern theology. We must examine it more closely.

It is in the relationship between history and consummation that Althaus desires to maintain both the connection and the break. But history as a being-in-time is for him as such a veiling and not an unveiling of the divine. Death is inherent in our temporariness. For that reason the Last Day is not a day in time, 'no history of the end but the history-ending event', so that this supra-historical reality will have no special relationship to the last earthly generation. Althaus sees here an insoluble antinomy, for time cannot be followed by eternity. This is contrary to the essence of eternity.[1] Niebuhr arrives at a similar conclusion. Talk of a certain point in the future when time is replaced by eternity 'is the cause of most of the literalistic corruptions of the Christian conception'.[2] Brunner discusses the matter under the title, 'Das Paradox der Endgeschichte' (The Paradox of the History of the End).[3] Platonism is for him too timeless in its concept of eternity, while Jewish apocalyptic thinks too much in temporal categories. He wishes to hold to both in order to approach the unexplainable.

Berdyaev thought much about these matters, and came to the same conclusion. He wishes to be neither Platonist, nor spiritualist. He wants to appreciate time and history positively. But time and sin belong together. Like Brunner he speaks of 'paradox' when he thinks about the future consummation and the manner in which the Revelation of John discusses it.

> The end of history is not an historical event. The end of time is not an event in time. The end of the world will not take place in the future, which is a part of our decrepit time. The end of the world is the end of time. Time will cease to exist. Time is a mark of the fallen state of the world.[4]

The closing words of his *The Meaning of History* read, 'The time has come for its [history's] profound reintegration as a moment in the everlasting mystery of the Spirit.'[5] With the possible exception of the last strong sentence, the described manner of speaking concerning time and eternity is widespread among Christian scholars. It is clear, however, that no one wishes to draw this way of thinking to its natural conclusions.

It is impossible to continue this line of thinking if one wishes to remain Christian in one's thought. There would then no longer be any question of consummation. History and timeless eternity are two totally different realities, which by definition have no common meeting ground. But it is essential to the biblical witness that history and consummation meet. They must meet in such a way that the latter is the extension of the first. For that reason the scholars mentioned above stop half-way, and take refuge in such terms as 'antinomy' and 'paradox'. There is, however, no antinomy here. Antinomy is created only when one thinks of the consummation as a timeless eternity in Platonistic terminology. But there is no reason to do this.[6]

A sharp reaction to Platonism came from Oscar Cullmann in his book *Christ and Time*.[7] It was obvious to him, as a reader of the Bible and as an exegete, that according to the Scriptures the future world is situated in time even as our world is. What we call eternity is another form of time and is nothing other than 'endless time' (p. 46). The New Testament term 'aeon' signifies limited time as well as what we call eternity; terminologically there is thus no difference between time and eternity (p. 62). Time as such, then, has nothing to do with sin. But Cullmann goes one great step further. Time is not even bound to man and creation. The eternity of God is nothing less than endless time, and our time is a limited part of it (p. 62).

No matter how grateful we might be that Cullmann broke the barrier to a Christian concept of eternity, the last statements seem suspicious to us. It seems that the boundaries between God and man are erased, and that God, together with us, is subject to the god 'Time' who surrounds both him and us. Our suspicions are perhaps unfounded. This could become evident only through Cullmann's definition of 'time'. But this definition is missing. It is obvious that Cullmann thinks of a progress from the past which is left behind, via a present which strictly speaking has no extension, to a future in which we have as yet no part. But it is immediately clear that we cannot talk this way about God's eternity. We cannot talk this way about the time of Christ, either. We are reminded of his pre-existence, of the fact that the future was anticipated in his appearance, and of a statement such as, 'Before Abraham was, I am' (John 8.58). In his fourth chapter, Cullmann discusses these New Testament elements. He has great difficulty in giving them a place in his linear concept of time. A very unlinear attitude to time seems to be expressed in the predestination and pre-existence of Christ, but this 'signifies nothing else [!] but that he, the Eternal One, is in control of the entire time line in its endless extension' (p. 72). At the same time it is stated that in Christ, as the centre of the time line, all that goes before has been fulfilled, and the future has been decided, so that in Christ 'the end is even now anticipated' (p. 73). It is clear that such realities can no longer be understood in the categories of what Cullmann calls a 'naive' conception of time. In its own way this is also true of the consummation.

Cullmann's opinion has been a wholesome corrective. But it is so much a reaction that it presents no solution. If we apply these controversies to our subject, we might say that in the same way that the first group leaves no room for the connection between this world and the consummation, so Cullmann does not do justice to the break, that is, the peculiarity of the consummation in relation to history.

Karl Barth introduced a concept of the relationship between time and eternity which avoids the Scylla of the contrast between the two, as well as the Charybdis of their identification.[8] Barth sees what we call time as being closely connected with sin. In our experience of time we no longer have the past, we do not yet have the future, and, therefore, we do not yet have a present either. Our time is that we never have time. But in Jesus Christ God took time, his time, for us. Christ also, as man, really had time. This 'fulfilled time' was revealed in our midst particularly during the forty days between the resurrection and ascension. Fulfilled time means that past, future, and present are revealed anew in their unity without losing their differentiation. Fulfilled time is also the representation of God's time, which we call eternity, in which past and future are connected in an eternal present. The individual who shares in Christ receives even now a small beginning of that fulfilled time because the atoning work of Christ has become his past which moves along through time and determines his present, and also because the Kingdom of God becomes his future which already has come near in the present.

In my opinion Barth has developed a conception of the problem of time, which escapes the aberration of both of the preceding views, and which also opens fruitful perspectives for our subject (which Barth does not discuss in these volumes).⁹ I would like to present this in my own words:

Time is the mould of our created human existence. Sin led to the fact that we have no time, and that we spend a hurried existence between past and future. But the consummation as the glorification of existence will not mean that we are taken out of time and delivered from time, but that time as the form of our glorified existence will also be fulfilled and glorified. Consummation means to live again in the succession of past, present, and future, but in such a way that the past moves along with us as a blessing and the future radiates through the present so that we strive without restlessness and rest without idleness, and so that, though always progressing, we are always at our destination. This is a stammering attempt to express what is above our experience, but it is no arbitrary stammering. It is grounded in the manner in which Jesus Christ (who is the same yesterday, today, and forever) has even now begun to give us time, in the lives of his believers as well as in history—in history because he delivered us from the unending cycle of naturalistic time, and keeps us from a senseless rush through an aimless, secularized time. He changes events into history because the liberating power of his sacrifice and resurrection move with us in our historical existence, and because we see the coming Kingdom dawn over us in the new reality created by it. This is true also for those who do not understand and confess it. Since we live 'after Christ', and since he has become the mystery of history, past, present, and future have approached one another in a manner which we may call a foretaste of the consummation.

The Connection Between History and Consummation

The above has made it clear that in view too of the relationship between time and eternity we cannot discuss the consummation as though it were merely the end of history. For the consummation also takes place within the bounds of time.

With this consideration in mind we may ask the last question which should occupy us: Can we discuss this question more concretely and more fully? Can we point out forces and figures in the history unshackled by Christ which will later be component parts of the glorified world?

On the bases of the preceding considerations this question is not presumptuous. This is certainly not the case when we remember how it is urged upon us by the figurative language of the Bible, which presents the relationship between now and later as that of sowing and reaping, ripening and harvest, kernel and ear. Paul states that a man can build upon Christ, the foundation, with gold or silver, so that his work will remain in the consummation and he will receive reward (I Cor. 3.14). The book of Revelation mentions the works which will follow the believers in the consummation (14.13), and twice it is said in the description of the new Jerusalem that the glory of the kings of the earth (21.24) and of the nations (21.26) will be brought into it. For us who must choose and labour in history it is of great importance to try to understand more clearly the meaning of this figurative language which speaks so plainly about a continuity between present and future.

Wherein is this continuity to be found? Our first and at the same time the most proper answer must be that it is found in the faithfulness of God, who does not leave incomplete what he has begun. Here again it is as in the individual's life. He who is my Redeemer is the guarantee that I will be resurrected. But the moment we realize this, our confession goes further. The Heidelberg Catechism states 'that since I now feel in my heart the beginning of eternal joy, I shall possess, after this life, perfect blessedness' (answer 58). Included in this is the fact that the faithfulness of God is revealed in the maintenance and glorification of certain realities which are already present in a small beginning; in this case the eternal joy. In regard to history, God's faithfulness is also revealed in the maintenance and glorification of the powers of the resurrection which are even now active.

But our thinking wishes to go beyond these general expressions. Do they mean that along with men certain structures and achievements will also be saved? Does the new world so build upon what we call a technical, political, or moral progress that those who are now in the service of the resurrection forces are gathering building materials for the glorified world? We know that the resurrection forces which are already active will later create the new world. But we ask: Will this be done with the results which are already attained?

Congar, a representative of that French Roman Catholic theology of history which accentuates the cross, and thus the break, gives a negative answer to this question, and by way of explanation uses the following illustration. A teacher assigns a very difficult set of problems to a student. The student does his best, but does not find the solution, although he more or less approaches it. Yet, his effort is not senseless, for he would never have developed his ability if he had received the solution immediately. The teacher finally gives him the solution, but only after he has in a certain sense become mature enough to receive it.[10]

But this answer is not entirely satisfactory. No matter how man himself might be held responsible, the answers given in history find their origin either in the Kingdom of God or in that of evil. The positive answers are the marks of Christ's dominion. Thus, there must be a greater connection with the future solution than Congar presents here.

Abraham Kuyper, too, struggled with this question; this was especially intense in his masterly work *De Gemeene Gratie* (Common Grace). He is generally very hesitant to speak about a direct connection. Continuity is found in 'the hidden germ of life' which will soon come to bloom. We are then spiritually mature, and the toy which helped us on the way is thrown out. He wants to explain the 'bringing in' of the glory of the nations into the New Jerusalem in such a way that the 'powerful germ', which is the basis of all, receives a new form from God. But he later quotes Paul's words in which the difference between now and later is compared with that between child and man (I Cor. 13.11f.).

He then discusses a direct connection; the greater is 'added to' the smaller part of the present so that the earthly 'remains, produces after-effects, joins in'. This is true especially of our rule over nature.

If an endless field of human knowledge and of human ability is now being formed by all that takes place in order to make the visible world and material nature subject to us, and if we know that this dominion of ours over nature will be complete in eternity, we may conclude that the knowledge and dominion we have gained over nature here can and will be of continued significance, even in the Kingdom of glory.[11]

In Kuyper, then, we find two possibilities in almost the same breath. Without choosing, G. J. Heering consciously places these together when he says this about the positive achievements of culture: 'Perhaps they are the scaffolding which may fall away when the House has been built. Perhaps God can and will also use them in his Kingdom.'[12] Althaus is somewhat more positive. 'Who will not refer the objective, spiritual content of history to a new "world" which is entirely the organ and the possession of the Spirit?'[13] And Daniélou says:

The new heaven and the new earth will be the transfiguration of this world, such as the work of man will have contributed to constitute it. In this sense the history of civilization as that of the cosmos enters into the total compass of the history of salvation.[14]

We join ourselves to these more positive expressions. The witness of Scripture concerning the connection between history and consummation is so forceful and certain, and the break between the two so serves this connection, that we are forced into the grateful acknowledgment that in the glorification of his world God will add to what has already been realized of the liberation of human existence. We purposefully express ourselves so generally. The children's song rightly says, 'Whatever is done in love for Jesus, keeps its worth and will remain.' This verse does not say too much. But it does say much too little. For it places too much emphasis on the subjective factor of our love for Jesus, and too little on the power of Jesus to reign in the midst of his enemies in order through this power to draw many, without knowing him, into the service of the deliverance of life which he came to bring. The fruit of *that* service, too, keeps its worth and will remain.

Since the outpouring of the Spirit, and since events are changed into history, the building materials for the glorified world are being gathered. One day God will add to this work of his Spirit. But then we must say that that upon which the building continues cannot be compared with that which is being built upon it. This double confession makes us grateful, and at the same time it humbles us.

NOTES

[1] Paul Althaus, *Die Letzten Dinge*, Gütersloh, 1949, pp. 250-55, 337-40.

[2] Reinhold Niebuhr, *The Nature and Destiny of Man*, London, 1946, vol. II, p. 310.

[3] E. Brunner, *Das Ewige als Zukunft und Gegenwart*, Zürich, 1953, pp. 143-48; English: *Eternal Hope*, London, 1954, pp. 130-35 (translation at fault).

[4] N. A. Berdyaev, *Dream and Reality: an essay in autobiography*, London, 1950, pp. 294f.

[5] Berdyaev, *The Meaning of History*, trs. G. Reavey, London, 1936, p. 206.

[6] Rev. 10.6 is often called upon; KJV, 'there should be time no longer', *sc.* time to repent. (RSV, 'delay'.)

[7] Oscar Cullmann, *Christ and Time*, trs. Filson, Philadelphia and London, 1950/51, pp. 37-80.

[8] See *Church Dogmatics* I/2, §14.1 ('God's Time and our Time'); III/2, §47 ('Man in his Time').

[9] This does not exclude criticism. Can Barth's emphasis on the first coming of Christ as the fulfilled time do justice to the elements of salvation history and succession defended by Cullmann? I am reminded of the meaning Barth ascribes in this connection to the forty days, in which their lack of fulfilment and their pointing to the future are not sufficiently honoured.

[10] I found this illustration from *Lay People in the Church* (*Jalons pour une théologie du laïcat*) in L. Malevez, *op. cit.*, p. 238.

[11] See *De Gemeene Gratie*, Leiden, 1902, vol. I, pp. 454-94. These pages are still very impressive. The quotations were taken from pp. 455, 456, 461, 477, 483.

[12] *De Verwachting van het Koninkrijk Gods*, Arnhem, 1952, p. 244.

[13] *Die Letzten Dinge*, p. 348.

[14] *The Conception of History*, p. 176.

9

THE INTERPRETATION OF HISTORY

Until the end of everything, no phenomenon of history is either
absolute good or absolute evil.
D. Chantepie de la Saussaye, *La Crise Religieuse en Hollande* (1860),
p. 50.

Why should one not do in the history of nations what everyone
who believes in Providence does in contemplating the events of
his own life?
Groen van Prinsterer, *Nederlandsche Gedachten* (1832), Series I,
vol. III, p. 112.

Faith, Experience, Science

WHEN, AS Western Christians, we involve ourselves with
the matters discussed in this book, we cannot avoid asking
what we are going to do with it all. We are suspicious of
ideas which do not direct our existence or inspire our
activities. We have learned this from the Bible. At the same
time we have, as Westerners, the tendency to strain this
conviction to the extent that we disinterestedly lay aside
those insights and prospects whose advantageous effects are
not immediately seen. By doing this we fall into the danger
of cutting ourselves off from the comfort and joy which are
already included in together seeing and acknowledging
Christ as the meaning of history. But even if we appreciated
this in the fullest sense, our feeling of discomfort would not
be entirely removed by it. For this has still an essential and
deeper root than our activism. This root is the schism in our
existence. I shall explain this by placing it in a broader
context.

God's revelation is the sum of the deeds and judgments by which he creates, directs, cuts across, and changes our reality. Revelation does not take place in the abstract. In all its moments it is related to what we call in the widest sense our reality. In his revelation God is concerned with that reality. And in our reflections and activity we, too, are dealing with it. Here we are concerned particularly with the reflections. God created the world. Geology and biology, for instance, deal with that creation. In the light of revelation, man is the image of God, but he is also a fallen creature. Psychology and anthropology are concerned with the being of that man. God called Israel and sent Christ. Israel's religion and the person of Jesus of Nazareth fall into the confines of the history of religion. And, turning again to our own theme, God changes human events into history as an analogy of the cross and resurrection of Christ. But this reality is at the same time the object of historical research. These two approaches to reality are entirely different. Faith (in scientific form: theology) talks about the cross and resurrection, about goal-directedness, about the antichrist and consummation. But the science of history nowhere encounters these realities. It sees everywhere flowing transitions and endless connections. It views human events in the light of continuity, causality, and relativity.

Earlier, when the sciences were still little developed and when they were subordinate to theology, there was no possibility of such different approaches to the one reality. Geology and biology worked with Genesis, and the science of history worked with the book of Revelation. Even when scientific reflection discovered its own subject matter and arrangement, these were brought into the theological framework. Reality is one, and whatever God says about it is scientifically decisive. But since the Enlightenment the sciences have been delivered from their subordination to theology, and have gone their own way. Each developed its own method in its approach to reality. In this way they all reached the kind of results which were attainable by their method. These results were entirely different from the biblical pronouncements about reality. The discoveries of astronomy and geology seemed to refute the story of creation, and those of the scientific study of religion seemed to refute the revelatory nature of Old and New Testament, and so on. At first (that is, in the eighteenth and particularly in the nineteenth centuries), these contradictions were noted with emotion: by the one side with horror, and by the other with exultation. Today, the relationship between faith and science is somewhat calmer. The practitioner of science is clearly aware of the fact that each department sees reality from only one point of view, and that for this reason many aspects of that reality must simply be left without consideration. The Christian Church has begun to understand that Scripture, too, is concerned with only one point of view—that of the relationship between God and our reality. We gradually realize (although in certain sections of the Church the degree of realization is still insufficient) that the Bible is not a textbook for astronomy, geology, and psychology, and so on. We now say, for instance, that the fact that God created the world is something quite different from what geology teaches us about the evolution of the earth in millions of years.

Indeed, it is something entirely different. Yet, by this the last word about the relationship between faith and science has not been said. For the witness of God the Creator is concerned with the same reality as that which interests geology. The latter deals with the work of creation! That this is the work of *creation* falls outside its field of vision; and the *work* falls in that field. But revelation illuminates this *same* reality and calls it creation. When we forget that it concerns the same reality, the judgments and deeds of God lose their concreteness. When we confess God as Creator, we may and must see the evolution (an evolution which was already suspected in Genesis 1) of heaven and earth before us. Faith and the experimental sciences do obtain differing points of view, but they are not contradictory—they are complementary. An all-inclusive intelligence could see all these points of view in their context, and in one glance could see reality in all its facets. But such intelligence is not allowed man in this existence. Yet, our thought and action cannot find rest in an unconnected plurality of viewpoints. Scholars will continue to suffer more and more under their specialization and the confusion of language that goes along with this. And the Church of Christ cannot rest in the fact that her confession regarding God's deeds and judgments becomes abstract because it is no longer related to her everyday experience of reality, nor is it related to the contemplations on reality by the sciences. God's deeds and judgments are related to this reality. They have a function in it. And our confession concerning it must be related to our experience of reality. It functions either here, or nowhere.

In the meantime, we are still in a time which fears combination more than division. It is different only in the field of the biblical sciences. In recent years there have been earnest attempts to bring into connection God's revelatory activities and the results of historical criticism. In that field such an attempt is ready at hand, but to bring into connection the doctrines concerning man and sin, and the insights of modern psychology is much more difficult. We are here talking about objectives for the future rather than tasks which simply can be begun now. But the wrong manner in which the churches for a long time imposed their pretended insights on science, and later placed these at least as a stumbling block on the road of research, left a fear which is still such a part of us that it is necessary to remind one another that this phase can only be an intermediate phase, which must be replaced by a new and thorough dialogue across the cleavages, and by building new bridges. The schism between revelation and experience, and thus between faith and science, has been of mutual refinement, which must lead, however, to a new encounter.

The Concept of History and the Facts of History

After this introduction we return to our actual theme. What we believe and confess concerning Christ as the meaning of history is related to the reality with which our history books are concerned. It *is* related to it; related to the reality established by God. But can we reflect upon it in such a way as to be able to describe that relationship? Can we identify here the negative and there the positive signs of Christ's dominion? Can we determine the exact line between good and evil, and penetrate to the very essence of history?

This is not possible. But *not* because the complexity of historical research would hinder us from drawing these conclusions from our confession. The cause of this lies in the content of the confession itself. For we confess that the Last Judgment, in which good and evil will be separated, is still before us, and that Christ alone will be the judge. We also confess that world history grows toward it and will lead to a clear, though still preliminary, separation of Christ's Kingdom and that of the opposing forces. Along with this we confess, however, that such a separation does not yet exist, and that it is not given to us to grasp for that great division which is brought by Christ alone.

Paul says that 'the mystery of lawlessness is already at work . . . then the lawless one will be revealed' (II Thess. 2.7f.). His future revelation implies that his activity in the present is a secret, a mystery. And when Jesus calls for watchfulness, the reason is, 'for you do not know when the master of the house will come' (Mark 13.35). It is true that we are moving towards a time of clearer division, such as was the case at the death of Jesus itself, and of both of those periods it is stated with emphasis that events will then be illuminated in the light of Jesus' words (Matt. 24.15, 25, 28, 33; John 13.19; 14.29; 16.4). But this assumes that such an illumination cannot be discussed outside of these critical periods. Without it our judgment about the manner in which historical facts are assimilated into the meaning of history will remain relative and provisional. This relativity is on our part not a timidity for which we need to apologize, or which we need to shout down by strong assertions, but it is the faithful reflection of the relativity of reality itself expressed so tersely by de la Saussaye, in the words at the beginning of this chapter.

But what then? Must we be silent and live in two worlds; one of a historical view of history, and a second, without connection with the first, of God's abstract judgments concerning that history? This cannot be the alternative. For relativity is not yet agnosticism. The fact that neither the Kingdom of Christ nor the kingdom of the antichrist has yet been revealed, but that they are hidden under the appearance of their opposite, and that they are everywhere intertwined, does not mean that nothing can be known or recognized of them. World history is not black or white, but it is not an even grey either. The eye of faith recognizes dark grey and light grey, and it knows that these gradual differences originate in differences of principle.

Added to this is a very important matter. History is the terrain of human decisions and actions. Choices must be made. We must live facing the great, coming separation, and in this way feed our fellow-servants (Matt. 24.45), keep the lamps burning, put the talents to usury, and help the oppressed (Matt. 25). These are the forms to be assumed by our watchfulness. We have seen that watchfulness arises from a lack of knowledge; but while waiting for the great, coming explanation, watchfulness must lead to choices, and so primarily to interpretation. He who watches must, for instance, be able to recognize his fellow-servants, and must know where the oppressed are in the world. He who watches interprets the facts. In view of the ambiguity of our history, every interpretation will always remain debatable. But it is unavoidable. It is an act of grateful obedience and as such is never meaningless and without blessing. It does not take place in a blind fashion. However relative the facts may be, the dark and light grey clearly press themselves into view. Of course, in this, too, subjective factors play their part. One draws back from the 'grey', while another is drawn to the 'light'. A uniformity of interpretation and decision can seldom be expected within the Christian Church. Our judgment remains, with the facts, relative. It does not coincide with the Last Judgment. It is infinitely more fallible than that. But it is of infinitely more meaning than not judging and not choosing. For it is the fruit of a faith that is awake; it is a work of thankfulness; and as such it is accepted and justified by God.

We find here a parallel to the manner in which the believer talks about God's leading in his personal life. That in the life of God's children all things work together for good is a matter of faith, and faith is an assurance of what one does not see. Faith is not dependent on vision, but it does lead to vision. It causes the believer to look for the signs of God's leading in his life. Sometimes he believes that he can see something of this leading, but later his interpretations may prove to be wrong. But that does not nullify that leading and faith. Along with this there are also interpretations which guide and direct a man's entire life. But what we do repeatedly for our personal life is even more true for the process of history in which we stand. For in that process man must constantly choose *for* the light grey and *against* the dark grey, and also against the grey *in* the light grey. He may and must do it there under penalty of becoming disobedient in his actions. At the same time he must not make his choice absolute under penalty of grasping in advance for the Last Judgment.

The Old and New Testaments are full of such interpretations of history. In this book we repeatedly pointed to the fact that the concept of history, especially in Daniel and Revelation, is not as indissolubly connected with contemporary events as is often supposed. The mysteriousness of the indications is more than a stylistic expression; it originates in the knowledge that in and behind events we are dealing with constantly recurring supra-historical constellations. But events are then still explained from this knowledge; and Antiochus Epiphanes and the Roman Empire are understood as the negative signs of God's dominion in history.

The Church has certainly recognized her distance from biblical prophecy, but this did not prevent her from interpreting her own time from the secret of history with the aid of the prophetic Word and guidance by the Spirit. It is noticeable, however, that in doing so she paid more attention to the negative than the positive signs. The first seem to force themselves to the attention more than the second. And in the second she often thought (too uncritically and at the same time too narrowly) only of herself. But the reversal in the Roman Empire under Constantine, the unified Christian culture from Charlemagne to the thirteenth century, and later the Reformation movement have by many been viewed as such positive signs. Among the things which in a very broad sense and for a long time have been considered to be negative signs the following are included: the Roman Empire before Constantine, Islam, the late-mediaeval Papal Court, the Turks, the Renaissance, the Enlightenment, the French Revolution, and in our own time National Socialism and Russian Communism.

With the inclusion of some of these examples we are immediately reminded of the relativity and, therefore, the fallibility of our interpretations. In the chapter, 'The Crucified Christ in History', we already mentioned the limitation of our interpretations. The Church all too quickly thought that she saw the maximum development of the antichrist himself present in the many antichristian appearances. Often God's work was uncritically identified with the work of the Church, or Satan was identified with the opposition, so that there was an eye neither for the antichristian tendencies in her own circles, nor for the changes which were taking place in the movements which had been labelled antichristian. For the dominion of Christ under which we live is particularly revealed in the fact that the demonic forces are not only called to life by him, but he also uses them, 'de-demonizes' them, and places them in his service. For that reason nothing is more dangerous in the necessary interpretation of history than dealing with fixed black and white stereotypes. On the one hand it leads to Pharisaism, and on the other to a lack of appreciation for Christ's power over his adversaries.

Let us look at an example of modern times. The majority of Christendom interpreted the French Revolution as being antichristian. In view of the many eye-catching slogans, theories, and practices there was enough reason for this. Yet, looking back we see that this interpretation remained tied to the surface of the phenomenon. Much which was considered to be essential disappeared; yet that which proved fruitful was often more Christian than antichristian. However, it took many years before Christendom was prepared for reinterpretation. Groen van Prinsterer developed an entire philosophy of history around the antichristian character of the French Revolution, which, because it is simple and handy, is still influential—although the leading figures of his present-day supporters have clearly pointed out that it is theologically and historically problematical. On the other hand, many believed around 1930 that Hitler must be appreciated as a positive force against the spread of Bolshevism and nihilism. Ten years later it would be clear to all that they had to do with an unmistakable antichristian phenomenon. It is no wonder that Communism is interpreted and attacked as antichristian. This is permissible as long as the attack is based not only on its materialistic atheism, but also at least equally on its view of man and its sacrifice of man to the goals of the idea. In the meantime it has become clear that Communism is susceptible to all kinds of changes and developments. Along with this we must also recognize the antichristian force in all the phenomena in the Western world which during the nineteenth century fed Communism, and which are still alive today in other forms: the glorification of labour, prosperity, and power coupled with a practical denial of God.

All this has been said to bring to our attention the hazardous undertaking of the interpretation of history. However, if that interpretation solidifies into a construction of fixed principles in a philosophy of history, it is overthrown. Interpretation demands a receptive heart and an open eye in order to see the continuous movements from light grey to dark grey, and *vice versa*, and accordingly to be ready constantly to revise one's own decisions. This also means that a man is aware of the relativity of his own view and that he considers other views possible—although it does not necessarily mean that he cannot enter into sharp debate with the supporters of other views and decisions. But when all this has been said and done, it must still be said that we cannot do without interpretation. Whoever does not interpret may have faith, but his labours in the field of history are dead.

Allow me to close this section by pointing to the magnificent pages where Karl Barth deals with these questions in his volume concerning Providence.[1] Barth warns against replacing faith in God's Providence by a philosophy of history. He then continues:

> In faith in God's providence man will certainly consider history with very open, attentive and participating eyes. How could it be otherwise? . . . It would not be faith if it were not knowledge in this respect, relative, provisional and modest knowledge in need of correction, yet true and thankful and courageous knowledge. When a man believes in God's providence, he does not know only *in abstracto* and generally that God is over all things and all things are in His hands, but he continually sees something of the work of this hand, and may continually see God's will and purpose in very definite events, relationships, connexions and changes in the history of created beings. He notes in this history disposings and directions, hints and signs, set limits and opened possibilities, threats and judgments, gracious preservations and assistances. He knows how to distinguish between great and small, truth and appearance, promise and threat. He knows how to distinguish between necessary waiting and pressing on, speech and silence, action and passion, warfare and peace. He perceives always the call of the hour, and acts accordingly.[2]

Of course (this is already clear from the quotation), Barth is aware of the fallibility of our observations and distinctions. With Bengel's view of history in mind he writes:

> We have to remember that there are fruitful as well as unfruitful misunderstandings of the Word of God. If the believer's

understanding is false in one respect, it is perhaps so much the better in others. And in any case it is better to misunderstand the Word of God than not to understand it at all.[3]

All things taken together, it is true that we do not have

the light in which all things are open to God. It is not the revelation and contemplation of *the* mystery, *the* history. But it is light, and as much light as God thinks necessary and salutary for the believer in his time and place, and will therefore give him.[4]

Interpretation and Attitude

On the one hand the Church of Christ is threatened by an easy white-black way of thinking, and on the other hand by scepticism. In both cases she wanders from the road of obedience. The sects with their massive, shortsighted, and often spiteful interpretations of present-day events identify faith and vision. But our answer is not found in a severance of the connection between faith and vision. Faith then becomes abstract, and vision is secularized. Thus we try to oust the devil by means of Beelzebub. We must take the courage to make relative decisions. We must look around, not only in the great world events in which our contribution is so small, but also in our own country and in our immediate surroundings, in order to discover and support the positive signs of Christ's dominion (even far outside the Christian Church), and to discover and oppose the antichristian tendencies (even in the heart of the Christian Church). For the meaning of our own life is fulfilled only when we take part in the meaning of history. Man can be a child of God without this, but he then merely exists or blindly reaches around in existence, driven on by his training, or by the spirit of the time, or by his daydreams. Paul says that he then builds wood, hay, and straw on Christ, the foundation. Such a one will be saved himself, but his work is burned. The important thing is that our work remains and that we receive our reward (I Cor. 3.10-15), so that the consummation will reveal that we have contributed to the formation of the

Kingdom which in Christ began to change and divide the world of man.

NOTES

[1] Karl Barth, *Church Dogmatics* III/3, pp. 21-26.
[2] *Ibid.*, p. 23.
[3] *Ibid.*, p. 25.
[4] *Ibid.*, p. 24.

EPILOGUE (1965)

As I announced in the Preface, the purpose of this short Epilogue is to indicate the position of this book and particularly of the chapters 2-4 in relation to the discussions and insights which arose in the years since the last revision of its Dutch edition. This Epilogue is especially meant for those who look at my book from the angle of theological expertise and progress. The division of the subjects is according to the order in which they appeared in the course of this book.

Old Testament

The main lines of my exposition in chapter 2 are in accordance with the dominant trends among present-day scholars. Von Rad's magnificent *Theology of the Old Testament* (1957, 1960; Eng. trs., 1962, 1965) found a world-wide echo and became the leading book. The discussion around this work refuted, corrected and limited several of its findings, but its basic lines are accepted by a large group of leading Old Testament scholars. In their approach the concept of history is central, because they consider Israel's faith as a belief in a movement of successive historical deeds by Yahweh, a movement which will find its continuation and completion in the future. The prevailing method of *Traditionsgeschichte* lays more stress on the difference between the layers of tradition than on the underlying unity (with important exceptions, e.g. Eichrodt and Zimmerli), this in contrast to the trend in my chapter 2. This does not affect, however, the broad agreement about the unique and fundamental place of history in Old Testament belief.

Epilogue (1965)

Apocalyptic

Scholars like Beek, Fritsch, and Rowley helped me to discern the theological relevance of the apocalyptic (chapters 2 and 3). Their positive judgment is still subject to controversy, however. Great scholars like Buber and von Rad reject it as not genuinely Israelite. I think that this attitude is due to dogmatic prejudice. How deeply the apocalyptic literature is rooted in the soil of the Old Testament the reader can see in the careful and detailed study of D. S. Russell, *The Method and Message of Jewish Apocalyptic* (London and Philadelphia, 1964).

It was a surprise to me that the theological relevance of apocalyptic was strongly expressed by New Testament scholars who discovered the positive role of this pattern of thinking in the belief of Jesus and of the primitive Church (Käsemann, Pannenberg and his school). I must also mention the name of Jürgen Moltmann. No one can hold this conviction without discovering sooner or later that a 'theology of history' of some kind is essential to every form of the Christian faith.

New Testament

The trend of my book and particularly of chapters 3 and 4 is irreconcilably opposed to the basic conceptions of the Bultmann school. According to this group a 'linear' understanding of God's deeds in history may be inherent in Old Testament faith; faith in Jesus Christ, however, implies that we are called to 'existence', which means *Entweltlichung*, i.e. being detached from the world and its horizontalities. Christ liberates us from law; he also liberates us from history as a linear horizontal movement to which we are subjected. Books and passages from the New Testament which give the impression that Jesus is the centre of a *Heilsgeschichte* (as is especially the case in the Lukan writings) are a relapse into an 'objectivistic' prechristian attitude.

This way of understanding Christ and the New Testament

is due to the philosophical presuppositions of Bultmann and his followers. Inspired by Heidegger they see a fundamental cleavage between the world of nature and history with their 'objectivizable' entities and the world of man, which means freedom and decision. As New Testament scholars of the Lutheran confession they often link this duality to Luther's strong emphasis on the Pauline contrast between 'Law' and 'Gospel', which are identified with the Old and New Testaments. In this way they radically de-historize the New Testament and limit the significance of Jesus Christ to that of the inspirer of existential life as it is confronted with God in the present. This is the most recent attempt in the long series which began with Gnosticism, to remould the gospel in accordance with the dominant philosophical ideas of the time.

We must distinguish, however, between the Bultmann school in the limited sense, to which belong all who consider the existentialistic philosophy the key to understanding the New Testament, and those who reject the hermeneutical significance of existentialism but follow Bultmann in the formal techniques of his New Testament studies, i.e. in the use of *Formgeschichte* and *Traditionsgeschichte* as the best method of discovering developments within the New Testament. This method deserved serious consideration by all who, like me, try to find out what was in the mind of Jesus and of his apostles.

But often this method is pushed far beyond its limits and is responsible for exaggerated results. For Bultmann and for many of his adherents most of the communications about Jesus go back not to Jesus himself but to the creativity of the first Christian community. Often there are good arguments for this opinion; more often, however, there is hardly any evidence. Besides, to the Evangelists who transmit the tradition, a very conscious and independent role in the *Traditionsgeschichte* is ascribed. The result is that the New Testament looks like a jungle of different and often contradictory traditions behind which the historical Jesus is almost completely hidden.

Epilogue (*1965*)

I cannot believe that the method applied can justify such results. The New Testament writings were written within a rather short period of time, in a small and simple community, separated by not more than a few decades from the happenings to which they testify, by people who had a deep concern for the pure transmission of the message. In no other field of history would such documents be treated with such scepticism.

Of course, the Gospels are not simply historical documents. They testify to a reality which is still present, to a Lord who is still speaking and acting among us through his Spirit. That is the reason why no sharp boundary-line can be drawn between the historical words of Jesus and the convictions of the first community, led by his Spirit. The Church could be creative in this field to a certain extent because she believed that Jesus as the exalted Lord remains present in the Spirit which leads her into all truth. (See the important preface of Günther Bornkamm's *Jesus von Nazareth*, 1956, Eng. trs. 1960.) But the community would have rejected any tradition about Jesus which they considered not in full accordance with the words and deeds of his historical life. I still therefore believe that the way in which I used the Gospels as sources in this book is more adequate than the distrust of their reliability which is now so widespread in Germany.

This conviction does not exclude the fact that were I to have to write my book today, I would have to dig deeper into some problems, particularly that of Jesus' messianic consciousness and titles. According to some of the German form-critics neither the title of the Suffering Servant nor that of the Son of Man was claimed by Jesus himself; both are applied to Jesus by the primitive Church. Particularly around the title 'Son of Man' a heavy battle is raging in which scholars like Bornkamm, Conzelmann, Käsemann and Vielhauer deny this title to the historical Jesus, whereas others like Cullmann, Dodd, Kümmel and E. Schweizer ascribe it to him. A good survey of the arguments of both groups is to be found in the theological encyclopaedia, *Die*

Christ the Meaning of History

Religion in Geschichte und Gegenwart: pro in the article 'Christologie I' by Sevenster, con in the article 'Jesus Christus' by Conzelmann. In my opinion the arguments of those who believe that Jesus did not use this title raise more problems than they solve. The process of tradition in the primitive Church included an element of creativity; but this creativity remained subordinate and subservient to the concern for faithful transmission.

Christ and History

Now it is evident why New Testament scholarship in Germany as the leading country (elsewhere it is quite different!) does not look favourably upon the connection this book makes between Christ and history: *Formgeschichte* is sceptical about the historical Christ; existentialism denies the relation between the gospel and 'linear history'. In spite of all this there are remarkable trends which indicate that this theme is too basic to the New Testament message to be neglected for long.

Ernst Käsemann in his famous article *Das Problem des historischen Jesus* (1954, in *Studies of the Historical Jesus*, London, 1964), strongly underlined, over against the Bultmann school in the restricted sense, the indispensability of the historical Jesus for the *kerygma*. Ebeling, Fuchs, and others, though belonging to the existentialist group, followed; according to their philosophy, however, they are inclined to limit the relevance of the historical Jesus to those words and deeds which seem to express a new conception of existence. Käsemann with his emphasis on the apocalyptic element in the gospel went beyond these limits (see above) and also other scholars, like Eberhard Jüngel and the American, J. M. Robinson, due to or in spite of their existentialist presuppositions, came to a wider appreciation of the element of history involved in the Christian *kerygma*.

At the same time a sharp counter-movement against Bultmann arose, originated by Wolfhart Pannenberg and his school (*Offenbarung als Geschichte*, 1961). According to this group revelation and linear history belong indissolubly together. German scholars are often inclined to extremes; this explains why Pannenberg and company, reacting against the Bultmann extreme, were in danger of neglecting essential elements of revelation which are beyond history (e.g. the relations of Word and Spirit, Faith and History). This movement is still developing and readjusting. Their strong point is the will to extend the Old Testament insights about God in history to the fields of the New Testament and dogmatics. In spite of several objections I believe it is important to watch this school, because their concern is justified.

In the meantime the existentialistic interpretation of the New Testament which is dominant in Germany, is widely rejected elsewhere, where the central place which the concept of history takes in the thought of Jesus and in the primitive Church is readily acknowledged and studied. I mention only three scholars whose works have strengthened my arguments: the Dane, Johannes Munck (*Paulus und die Heilsgeschichte*, 1954, Eng. trs. 1959), the Englishman, Alan Richardson (*An Introduction to the Theology of the New Testament*, London and New York, 1958; *History Sacred and Profane*, London and Philadelphia, 1964) and particularly the Swiss, Oscar Cullmann, whose latest book with its significant title, *Heil als Geschichte* (1965, Eng. trs., 1966) is the most elaborate exposition of the historical character of the New Testament in all its manifestations. Cullmann rightly points out that the existentialistic approach to the New Testament is not wrong, but has to be set into a wider historical context. The more carefully and objectively the self-understanding of man in the New Testament is studied, the more it will become clear, I am sure, that here man understands himself as finding his life in a great development outside of himself, history from creation to consummation, of which Jesus Christ is the centre, whose cross and resurrection are the key to the understanding of present and future.

Typology

When I wrote down my insights on repetition and typology, I was not yet acquainted with the discussion which had
already begun at that time in Protestant theology, about the
meaning and extent of typology (von Rad, Bultmann,
Zimmerli, Baumgärtel, Eichrodt, van Ruler, etc.). This
discussion has confirmed my ideas about the essential role
of typology in the Bible. However, I deplore that most
authors are mainly interested in those events (in the Old
Testament) which prefigure the appearance of Christ, and
far less in those events which are repeated in history before
and after Christ and are related to the *eschaton*. A study of
the mutual relations of the christological, ecclesiological, and
eschatological types would deepen our insight into the basic
function of typology, as well as its limits.

Secularization and Secularism

In recent years the close connection between Christianity
and secularization, treated here in chapter 5 and elsewhere,
has been expressed by many authors. I feel particularly
grateful for the impressive book by my fellow-countryman,
Arend Th. van Leeuwen, *Christianity in World History* (London, 1964). All thinkers on this subject wrestle with the
relation between the positive and the negative aspects of
secularization. English-speaking writers are inclined to distinguish these aspects by the words 'secularization' and
'secularism'. I wonder whether this verbal distinction is
very helpful in discovering the essential features of the two
aspects. Others distinguish between 'emancipation' and
'secularization'—which seems a better distinction to me. In
this book I used the phrase 'Christian' and 'antichristian'
secularization. I made the observation that many Christians,
impressed by the 'rapid social change' everywhere in the
world, are inclined to overemphasize the positive aspects of
this development and to underestimate the negative ones.
I hope that my exposition, though intentionally directed

against Christian pessimistic views of history, will help those others too to come to a more biblical conception, which is at the same time more two-sided and dialectical.

INDEXES

Index of Names

Index of Names

Vitellius, 129
Vitringa, C., 166
Vogel, H., 166

Werner, M., 79f.
Windelband, W., 27

Zahn, T., 129
Zarathustra, 19f., 27, 44, 54, 158
Zechariah, 45, 48f., 64, 136, 149
Zimmerli, W., 206, 212
Zündel, F., 179

INDEX OF REFERENCES

OLD TESTAMENT

Index of References

221